THE

FLOGGING-BLOCK

An Heroic Poem

in

A PROLOGUE AND TWELVE ECLOGUES

BY

ALGERNON CHARLES SWINBURNE

A Transcription

of

The Original Holograph Manuscript
Written at intervals between
1862 and 1881.

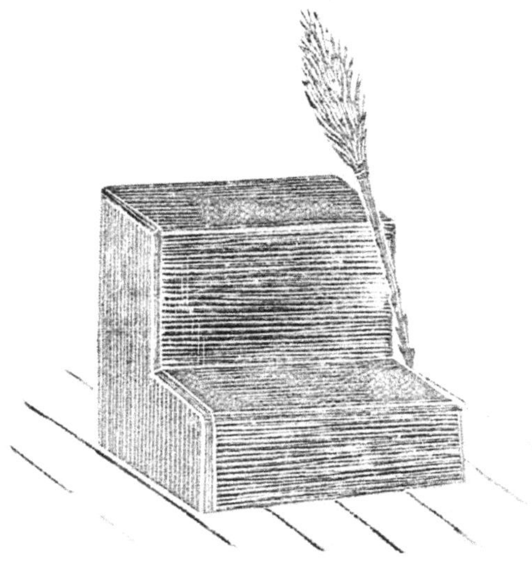

BIRCHGROVE PRESS
2011

ISBN:
978-0-9870956-9-5

The original holograph manuscript of *The Flogging-Block* is owned by the British Library. It is held in the Ashley Manuscripts collection (Ashley 5256). This edition was published with the kind permission of the British Library.

Transcription produced by Mark McDougal

http://www.birchgrovepress.com

info@birchgrovepress.com

The illustration on the cover and title page depicts the Eton flogging block. It is from the cover of *Flagellation & the Flagellants. A History of the Rod in All Countries From the Earliest Period to the Present Time* by the Rev. Wm. M. Cooper, B. A. (London: John Camden Hotten, 1870; Birchgrove Press, 2010). See also *Flagellation & the Flagellants*, p. 436, Plate XIX, 'The Rod in School', 'ETON FLOGGING "BLOCK" AND ROD.'

THE

FLOGGING-BLOCK

An Heroic Poem

CONTENTS

* The Eclogues in the table of proposed contents differ from those in the completed manuscript.

Preface

The primary aim of this volume is to present, for the first time, Algernon Charles Swinburne's hitherto unpublished manuscript, *The Flogging-Block. An Heroic Poem,* which was written at intervals between 1862 and 1881.[1] *The Flogging-Block* consists of a Prologue and twelve Eclogues on the corporal punishment of school boys with illustrations by Simeon Solomon. The original holograph manuscript is owned by the British Library and is held in the Ashley Manuscripts collection (Ashley 5256). I would like to express my gratitude to the British Library for granting permission to publish this edition, a page by page and line by line transcription of the manuscript.

Excerpts from *The Flogging-Block* have appeared in biographies and critical literature but the entire cycle of burlesque poems has remained unpublished until now. It is difficult to understand why it has not been made available. In an age where popular media is saturated with violent imagery, one can hardly justify the manuscript's neglect or suppression on the grounds that the violence associated with chastisement is repellent. Some readers may find Swinburne's representation of flagellation harrowing but it is far less disturbing than some of the brutal fare that passes for entertainment on cinema and television screens. It is not explicitly sexual and is tied to notions of honour, courage, and masculinity. Conceivably, it could be mobilised for anti-corporal punishment purposes.

Swinburne suggests that flogging causes the recipient profound distress but amuses and enchants the rod's wielder and its witnesses. It is not effective as a deterrent or corrective and leads to an escalating cycle of violence and brutality because it is pleasurable to watch and inflict and provides the sufferer with an opportunity to demonstrate his fortitude or "pluck" and thus, evidence his moral worth. Swinburne lampoons the disciplinary use of the rod in elite Victorian schools such as Eton (where as a student he was almost certainly beaten) through exaggeration, by depicting masters as self-serving despots enthralled with birching, and by portraying students revelling in the punishment of their fellows.

Some readers may argue that *The Flogging-Block*, which contains numerous semi-autobiographical elements, should remain unpublished because its representation of the torments and delights of chastisement is indicative of sexual perversity; hence, its publication may damage Swinburne's reputation as a major Victorian poet. This argument is specious because Swinburne's penchant for the rod is well-known.[2] Flogging scenes abound in his published and unpublished poetry, fiction, letters, and dramatic works, and he is known to have frequented at least one brothel specialising in flagellation. Swinburne's literary standing, therefore, is most unlikely to be tarnished by the publication of another work of his involving corporal punishment, and especially if, like *The Flogging-Block*, it does not contain overt sexual content.

---

[1] *The Flogging-Block*'s correct title is unclear. The British Library's manuscript catalogue describes Ashley 5256 as "'The Flogging Block': a burlesque heroic poem by A. C. Swinburne; circa 1862-1887." The manuscript's title page, which may not have been written by Swinburne, states: "THE / FLOGGING-BLOCK / An Heroic Poem / in / A PROLOGUE AND TWELVE ECLOGUES / BY / ALGERNON CHARLES SWINBURNE / With Illustrations / by / SIMEON SOLOMON / The Original Holograph Manuscript / Written at intervals between / 1862 and 1881." On the first page of the Prologue, in Swinburne's hand, the title appears thus: "The / Flogging-Block. / An Heroic Poem. / By Rufus Rodworthy, Esq. / (Algernon Clavering) / With Annotations / By Barebum Birchingham, Esq. / (Bertram Bellingham) / London: / 1777." In the bibliography to Ian Gibson's *The English Vice: Beating, Sex and Shame in Victorian England and After* (Duckworth, 1978), the manuscript's title is recorded as *The Flogging-Block. An Heroic Poem. By Rufus Rodworthy, Esq. (Algernon Clavering) With Annotations By Barebum Birchmore, Esq. (Bertram Bellingham) London: 1777.*

[2] Swinburne's enthusiasm for flagellation is well-documented. A comprehensive but not particularly sophisticated account of it is found in Gibson's *The English Vice*. For an excellent biography of Swinburne, see Rikki Rooksby, *A. C. Swinburne: A Poet's Life* (Scolar Press, 1997).

As a creative work, *The Flogging-Block* is worth publishing because it is a manifestation of an important writer's abiding passion, which was shaped but not necessarily caused by his boyhood experience of scholastic discipline. It is not high art — it does not reach or evidence an effort to attain the lyrical and metrical brilliance of Swinburne's best work — but is worth reading. *The Flogging-Block* often captures, with considerable vigour and marked black humour, the ostensible torture, anguish, and delight of castigation. Swinburne must have valued it because, although he does not appear to have intended it for publication, he spent almost twenty years writing it. *The Flogging-Block*'s publication is also merited because it is probably the longest English poetic work focusing on flagellation in scholastic contexts, which makes it significant for studies of the social, cultural, and historical development of flagellant literature and clandestine erotica. It comprises 92 folios, many of which are written on both sides, and totals over 42,000 words. By way of contrast, *The Rodiad* (1871), which is a fairly long poem exploring similar terrain that was published clandestinely by Swinburne's publisher, John Camden Hotten (it was probably written by Swinburne's friend and mentor, Richard Monckton Milnes, later Lord Houghton), is just over 3000 words.

This first edition of *The Flogging-Block* does not pretend to be definitive. It omits Solomon's fine illustrations and the transcription of the text, which is based on copies of the manuscript supplied by the British Library, is incomplete. Occasional words and lines could not be read because of what appears to be fading in the original and because of difficulties interpreting Swinburne's handwriting. The chorus in 'Eclogue I' and 'Edgar's Flogging' have the greatest concentrations of illegible words and lines. It may be possible to recover some of the text by using more sophisticated imaging techniques than those employed to produce the copies on which this transcription is based. Greater familiarity with Swinburne's hand may enable the correction of transcription errors and omissions resulting from interpretative difficulties. It is possible that some illegible sections of text could be recovered by examining the original manuscript, which was beyond the means of this project, or by locating copies or transcriptions that were made before the present state of apparent fading occurred. One of the main hopes of this edition is that it will stimulate interest in *The Flogging-Block* leading to the publication of an authoritative edition with a comprehensive scholarly introduction and Solomon's illustrations. With the aim of producing the best possible edition, we invite readers to submit corrections and transcriptions.

Mark McDougal.

Notes on the Transcription

This edition is a page by page and line by line transcription of the holograph manuscript. It approximates the layout of Swinburne's text in order to facilitate comparison with it. Manuscript margins are fairly small because the poet varied the size of his handwriting and line spacing to fill each sheet of paper. In the transcription, it was not feasible to vary formatting to produce a similar effect. In order to reproduce variations in line number and line length accurately and produce a transcription with a reasonable font size throughout, it was necessary to produce a fairly large format book: 8.5 by 11 inches. This has resulted in a larger than desired margin at the bottom of most pages.

In the manuscript, folio leaves are not numbered consecutively throughout. Swinburne's numbering, where legible, is transcribed in the upper right corner of the page. Page numbers of this edition are printed at the bottom of the page in the centre.

Illegible words and lines are indicated by an ellipsis enclosed by square brackets:

'And the birch [...] makes it smart' ('Eclogue I')

Words and phrases appearing within square brackets are conjectural:

'Don't you wish you [could pull] down your shirt?' ('Eclogue I')

In the manuscript, emphasis is indicated through underlining and the use of larger print. The transcription underlines words underlined in the original and indicates apparent emphasis by increasing font size and the use of bold formatting. Where Swinburne uses significantly smaller handwriting to add text or make revisions, the transcription employs smaller font sizes. Deleted text, where legible, is transcribed with a strikethrough:

'~~You wonder how he deigns to speak~~' ('Reginald's Flogging': 'Another Epilogue')

Many of the poems tally birch cuts at the beginning or (more frequently) the end of each line. Where these numbers are legible, they are represented in the transcription by reductions in font size or through superscript and subscript. They should not be confused with footnotes or endnotes, which occur only in the Prologue ('Note to "Algernon's Flogging"' is not referenced within Eclogue I.)

The table of contents at the beginning of this edition is based on the manuscript's typewritten contents table, which precedes the Prologue, the first page of the manuscript that appears to be in Swinburne's hand.

THE

FLOGGING-BLOCK

An Heroic Poem

The

Flogging-Block.

An Heroic Poem.

By Rufus Rodworthy, Esq.
(Algernon Clavering.)

With Annotations

By Barebum Birchingham, Esq.
(Bertram Bellingham)

London:
1777.

[1]

I sing the Flogging-block. Thou, red-cheek'd Muse, [1]
Whose Hand the Blood of smarting Boys' imbues,
Scholastic Dame, revered of Church & State,
Whose Lords to be have writhed beneath the Birch,
Thou that canst see, & smile, before thy Frown
A budding Bishop takes his Breeches down,
And, tingling at the Terrors of thy nod,
A Judge that shall be Strip to taste the Rod,
And ere his Brow be ripe for Boys to come
Birch, Birch entwine [2] the beardless Poet's Bum,
Birch, Birch alone embrace his brawnier Part,
Birch, Birch inflame his Flesh with constant Smart,
Birch, daily Birch, [3] ring Music in his Ears,
Birch, hourly Birch, [4] renew his recent Tears,
Birch, Birch, incessant Birch, [5] fill all his Days with Fears:

Thou that hast whipp'd so many a boyish Bard
So soundly, & so often, & so hard,
(For chief the Stripling Songster's Breech invites
The full Performance of they frequent Rites, [6)]
And most the Nurslings of the Muse require
The Lash that sets their lyrick Blood on Fire,
The Lash that ever when they cry keeps Time,
When Stroke to Stroke responds in glowing Rhyme,
And still the humbled Bottom hails the Rod sublime,
Till Heart & Head the rhythmic Lesson learn
From wounds that redden & from Stripes that burn,
As Twig by Twig imprints the Crimson Sign in turn,
Till, faint with Fear, bowed Head & trembling Heart
Learn of the Bottom, of that Lowliest Part,
The Lesson learnt & taught at once with Shame & Smart,
Till all the Rods that whipping Pedants use
Through all their Blood the kindling Pain infuse
That stings the stalwart Bum, & wakes the sluggish Muse;[7)])
Thou that has made the Warrior yet to be
Whine at each Wound in Battle given of thee,
Shrink at the shrill reverberating Shock
When Birch & Bottom battled on the Block,
And wince to see the Weapon raised, or hear
The sound of switching Twigs invade his ear;
If ever at thy daily dreadful Shrine
My votive Bum has offered Blood of mine, [8)]
Inspire the burning Song, inflame the living Line.

She hears! she hears! Already on mine Eyes
Scenes once but too familiar seem to rise:
Again I see & shudder at my Doom,
The dark high Precinct of the Flogging-Room:
The Block so long familiar to my Knee,
The Birch to none more cruel than to me;
With Arm raised high I see my Master stand
And grasp the brandished Rod with sinewy Hand:
The supple Twigs, the swelling Buds I view,
That once too well my burning Buttocks knew:
But who is he, the bare-breeched Boy there kneeling? Who? [9)]
With visionary Eye reversed I see
Myself in him, & gaze myself on me.
I see the Shirt drawn up, the Bottom bared,
The Bottom daily Stripped and never Spared: [10)]
I see my Stripes, I see the numerous Weals
That prove what pain my Bum each morning feels,
I see my Breeches hanging loose about my Heels:
I see where most the recent Rod has hurt:
I see, tenacious of the lifted Skirt,
My Brother & my Cousin holding up my Shirt: [11)]
I see them smile & leer upon other;
Ah cruel Cousin! Ah the more cruel Brother! [12)]
The piercing Pain my tender Bum endures
Adds Pleasure to the Painlessness of yours:
Each Pang that thrills my Buttocks through & through,
Torture to me, is Ecstasy to you. [13)]

And now no more I see: [14] for now I feel
The Rod salute my Bottom as I kneel,
And raise at every Stroke a fresh great smarting Weal.
I feel once more each Twig, each Knot, each Bud,
Sting my soft Flesh & fire my fevered Blood;
I feel the Stripes behind me burn & throb;
I smart, I writhe, I groan, I moan, I sob,
I wince, I flinch, I howl, I roar with pain, [15]
'And weep the more because I weep in vain.'
And still the Birch-Twigs ply my Bum afresh,
And still the Torment rages in my Flesh.
Now, tho' my Cheek the burning Tears besmirch,
My Torturer call for yet another Birch:
And while my Breech expects another Dozen
I hear my Brother whisper to my Cousin —
'Ah! won't the Youngster's Bottom smart, by G— !
Ah! won't it blush & redden from the Rod!
His Flagellation is but now begun:
He'll have enough to cry for ere 'tis done:
The Birch itself delights to whip young Alg-rn-n.' [16]
I hear my Cousin whispering to my Brother —
'This was a good tough Rod — but see the other!
See, Charlie, what a lithe, fresh, sappy one!
I call your Brother's Flagellation Fun:
I like to see the Birch-Twigs tickling Alg-rn-n.'
I hear, & feel the second Rod begin
With Stroke on Stroke to play upon my Skin.

5

I cannot cry: my Throat is chok'd with Sobs:
Like throbbing Fire my smarting Bottom throbs.
Each Lash renews the Torture: all in vain
I turn my Head & lifting my Eyes up, fain
To win some little Pity for my piteous Pain.
Hard as the hard old wooden Flogging-Block
The faces are, that meet my Face & mock:
My Cousin chuckles, & my Brother grins,
To see their Junior suffering for his sins:
At Each fresh Birchen Stroke they smile afresh
To see 'the young one' suffer in the Flesh.
Each time the Twigs bend round across my Bum
Pain bids 'Cry out,' but Honour bids 'Be dumb.'

Notes to ‘The Flogging-Block.’

By Barebum Birchingham.
(Bertram Bellingham).

1) ‘Red-cheek’d Muse.’ The Muse who presides over the Ceremony of Flagellation & inspires the Song which attempts to celebrate the Flogging-Block, is so styl’d from the Hue produced by the first Strokes of the Rod on the nether Cheeks of the Boy chastised — ‘his nether Cheeks full broad & white’ when first exposed to the Lash, but after a few good hearty Strokes (well applied with a good smart Rod) all suffused with a glowing Crimson; from whence as by Reflection the face of the Goddess of Whipping may be supposed to catch Fire, & take colour from the blushing Backside of the naked Boy whose Flesh does Penance in her Sight on the Birchen Altar of the Whipping-Block.
2) The Birch may be said to clasp or entwine the Bum of the flagellated Youth (as Wreaths of Bay or Laurel the Head of a Conqueror or a Poet), seeing how at each Cut of the Rod the birchen Twigs bend round the Youngster’s naked Haunches & twine themselves about his Flesh in a stinging Embrace.
3) Birch is the daily Fare of Truants or Idlers. The Flogging Lists of any School will show this.
4) Birch may be said to be the hourly Fare of such as will not submit their Irregularity of Spirit or Insubordinacy of Temper to any other but only the Birchen Discipline of the School: so that they never know on coming into School (tho’ it be four or five or six Times a Day) whether they will not be well whipt before they come out again. I have known a young Gentleman of good Family & good parts severely Whipp’d no less than seven Times in one Day, receiving at each Bout eighteen smart lashes on his bare Breech

with a Couple of fresh green sappy new Rods, so that his tender Backside was wellnigh cut to Pieces: his Fault being, first, that he fail'd of saying his morning Lesson; for which he was sharply Chastis'd at eight o'clock; secondly, that after Whipping he answer'd very Impertinently to a Jest that the Schoolmaster crack'd on his pitiful smarting Condition; for which he was immediately Chastised again, & more Severely (if this was Possible) than before; thirdly, that about two Hours later he was taken out of Bounds, & brought in by a Deputy of the School whose Office it was to lay wait for such Trespassers: for which he was so severely Whipped that when at length the Schoolmaster laid aside his [sturdy] Instrument his Arm was too weary to Flog another Boy (who was therefore Respited till the next Day); fourthly, at being shortly afterwards in the Playground, much Baited & [...] by his Schoolfellows on account of the Whippings his Breech had already received, he struck & fought with the Prefect or Deputy who had laid [...] on him while playing Truant & brought him back to receive Correction: for which Offence he was yet more severely Flogged than for all his Faults preceding, insomuch that his Bottom was now covered all over with bloody Weals:

fifthly, that after being thus Chastised he went (without Leave
given of his Master) to bathe in the River adjoining the School
Playground, there to cool the Smart of his Stripes & ease the
burning & fiery Pain of his whipped Posteriors; for which he
was again so sharply Flogg'd that all his Punishment
already received seemed less than the Correction now administered
by a stout Pair of strong & supple Birchen Rods: sixthly,
that he was Fain to excuse himself for neglect of his Task
in the Afternoon, on the Score that he was unable to apply
himself to his Book, his Mind being distracted from it
by the Smarting of his five time whipp'd Posteriors;
for which he was instantly Whipp'd again, & received so
severe a Correction that he Cry'd & Whin'd aloud for Mercy
at every Stroke of the Rod; yet was all his Crying in vain; for
his Schoolmaster plied his Bottom so heartily with the Lash
that at every Encounter between the tough Twigs of the Rod
and tender Flesh of the Stripling a small Stream of Blood
would gush forth from Wounds yet unhealed: seventhly, that after
all this he was wellnigh half an Hour late at Evening School; for
which he was so severely Flogged, that his Punishment alone
might have sufficed to expiate all those Transgressions for
which his Posteriors had already smarted so sharply, & worn
out already Twelve new supple stout Birch Rods: yet now two
more were most heartily applied to the Wealed & Bloody Breech
of the Flagellated Stripling. (This experience occur'd at School to Mr. A. Clavering
the Author of this Poem) on the Day on which he completed his fifteenth or sixteenth year.

The Flogging-Block. Eclogue I. Algernon's Flogging.

Scene – The public flogging room.
Schoolmaster. Algernon. George. Leonard. Arthur. Reginald. Percy.

Francis. Edward. Wilfred. The Rod.

Master. Come here, Master George, take Algernon's breeches down;
(Holding Algernon by the collar.
And you, Master Reginald, hand me the switches down,
The tough birchen switches that keep the school jogging;
And I'll give Master Algy a thorough good flogging.
(Shaking Algernon by the collar.
A thorough good flogging shall Algernon get;
His posteriors have never been whipped enough yet.
So in sight of his equals in age & superiors
(George begins unbuttoning Algernon's trousers.
I'll do justice on Algernon's naked posteriors.
I'll cut up his buttocks; I'll tickle his hide;
(Reginald comes forward with a stout birch rod.
With a thorough good flogging I'll warm his backside.
(George leaves Algernon's trousers half unbuttoned.
See, boys, how he blushes! how red his cheeks are!
(Algernon takes down his trousers, and kneels down on the flogging-block.
But his other end soon shall be redder by far.
(George takes up Algernon's shirt.

Reginald. Here's a jolly good birch, sir, just fresh from the pickle.

Master. Aye — there's a big brawny bare bottom to tickle.
Ah, you know what the birch is — eh, Algernon, eh?
(Shaking the rod over Algernon's naked bottom.

Algernon. Oh, don't whip me this once, sir — not much, sir — oh pray —

Edward. O, shan't we just see a good swishing, by God!
It's all wet from the brine — what a stunning great rod!

Arthur. It's all knotty & supple & pliant & lithe —
O, I say, won't it make Master Algernon writhe!

Wilfred. Don't it just look a stinger, I say, my boys, don't it?
Oh, & won't it cut bits out of Algernon — won't it?

Reginald. There are just seven twigs, & each twig is in bud —
And I'll bet you the very first cut will draw blood.

Frank. Well, I'm sorry for Algy, but still it's a spree;
[And] his floggings are always so jolly to see.

Percy. They're not jolly to get, though — I know what he feels;
His white skin will be soon one great mass of red weals.

Leonard. Every twig in the rod is green & so buddy,
The first twinge will leave Algernon's bottom all bloody.

George. Aye, by Jove, it's a tickler — stout, springy, & sappy —
I say, Algernon, tell me now, don't you feel happy?

Algernon. Don't chaff me just now, I say, George, there's a trump —

George. Can't you feel the first touch of it tickle your rump?
Don't the thought make you tingle before the strokes come?
Don't you feel the flesh creep, the blood burn in your bum?
Oh, I say, won't it sting you! by Jove, won't it hurt!

Master. Here, Edward, my boy, hold up Algernon's shirt.
You and George must between you — make sure that he shan't
Rub his bottom however it smarts — and he can't.
Ay, Redgie, this birch is a birch to my [...] —
(Edward holds up Algernon's shirt on the right — George holds it up on the left.
Now we'll see what you think of it, Algernon — Swish!
(Flogs Algernon.

Algernon. O, sir, how it stings! O you hurt me, you hurt!
Let me rub myself just with the end of my shirt. —
(The master flogs him again.
O, it cuts me again! O, sir, put down the birch!
O, please sir — I'll never shirk school or miss church —
(The master whips him soundly.
O, don't hit so hard, sir! I won't, sir — I won't!
(The master whips him very severely.
O, sir, the birch hurts me so awfully — Don't!
(The master flogs him soundly.
O, please sir, don't always hit just the same part!
(The master flogs him severely.
O, sir, you don't know how you're making me smart!
(The master laughs, & whips him again.
Oh, I'll never be late when the chapel bell rings —
(The master whips him very severely indeed.
O, sir, you can't think, you can't think how it stings!
(The master smiles, and whips him again and again.
O, please sir, I'll always do all that you wish —
O, that cut was like fire to my bottom, sir — Swish!

2

O, don't whip me so — anything rather than that! (The master flogs him again.
(Swish, swish, spat, spat, spat, swish — swish, swish, swish, swish, swish —
21 spat!)
O, it cuts me again, & again, & again!
O, I never yet felt such unbearable pain
All over my bottom & right up my back — (The master flogs him severely.
Swish — Swish — Swish — Swish — Swish — Swish — Smack — whack,
35 whack, whack, whack, whack!)
Oh, please, sir — oh, sir, you can't think how you hurt!
Let me just rub my bottom this once with my shirt!
O, I'll never play truant to shoot or to fish —
(Swish, swish, swish, swish, swish, swish, swish, swish, swish,
45 swish, swish, swish!) (The master flogs him [...]
O, I'll never break bounds, sir, to hunt or to ride.
But do, sir, for pity's sake, spare my backside!
O, sir, please, won't that do? I can bear it no more
O, you do hit so hard, & my bottom's so sore!
Oh, oh, oh! at each cut I can feel the blood trickle —
Master. Does it sting? does it hurt you my boy? does it tickle?
Can you boast that for you the birch rod has no terrors?
That your bottom don't mind it, when scourged for your errors?
(Flogging Algernon very severely indeed.
50 Take that, sir! & that, sir! — & that — that — & that!
Algernon. Oh please sir — Oh (Swish!) — Oh, you hurt me so — ([...]
(The master flogs him again and again.
58 (Swish!) Oh, I can't bear it. (Hursh — hursh — hursh — hursh —
Hursh) (The master flogs him more severely than ever.
62 Oh (swish) won't you — (swish) — let me — (swish) — get up — (swish)?
Oh, stop for one moment, & let me take breath!
Oh my bottom, my bottom! you'll flog me to death!

[…I.]

Chorus

Bare of breeches, bare of shirt,
How his bottom must be hurt!
Still the birch falls fast & hard
On the part no trousers guard;
Still as stroke to stroke succeeds,
How his bottom burns & bleeds!
Still the doctor whips it well,
Still the red stripes rise & swell;
Still the deep warm crimson dyes
All the tender part that lies
Naked to his […]:
Every fresh cut […]
The bare breech of Algernon
Makes the swelled flesh rise in ridges
Thick as […]
[…]
[…]
[…]
[…]
[…]
[…]
[…]
66 […]
Can those [broad] red […]
That […] blood [scores & streaks,]
That the [red rod…] & dapples
Like two great red […] streaked apples
That the birch twigs cut & […]!
How they [redden ain't] it nice!
[…] between the tender part
And the birch […] makes it smart
[…] between the smart to [deaden]

How his [buttocks] burn & redden!

[…I.]

No — he can't pull down his shirt —
No, not he — & don't it burn!
Fain would Algy rub is bottom
As, when birch [behind] has [got 'em],
Schoolboys all to rub are fain,
Rub the smart off — all in vain!
Vain, as all in time must find
When they're […] to […]
Doomed to […]
Feel what Algy's bottom [feels]
Tingling from those great red weals.
[…]
[…]
Spreads […]
[…]
[…]
[…]
[…]
[…]
[…]
[…]
[…]
[…]
[twists] & tingles, […]
[…]
[…]
[…] Algernon […]
[…]
Makes his […]
Thick & long & red & lurid
Weals inlay the flesh with […]
Stripes as deep as […] & […]
Stripes & ridges, scars & cuts

Epode 1.

69 Look at that! & that! & that!
76 Swish! Swish! Swish! Swish! [Spat!]
Spat! Spat!
Look, he's wriggling, like a fish —
83 Swish! Swish! Swish! Swish! Swish! Sw[ish!]

Algernon's Flogging. 3

Algernon (writhing & crying).
Oh, oh, oh, sir! Oh please, sir! Oh, oh, sir! Oh! Oh!
You don't know — you can't think how it hurts — you don't know!
Oh, please, sir, not there, sir! Oh, don't hit it there!

George. Oh, isn't it nice to see Algernon bare? (The master flogs Algernon again.
Oh, isn't his bottom a pattern when stripped!
Oh, it does one's heart good to see Algernon whipped!
Flog him well, sir! flog harder! that's it! make him wince!
Sing, Algernon, sing, sir! sing out like a prince!
Whip his bottom, sir — whip till the stripes [burn] and swell!
Whip him soundly! He flinches again — whip him well!
Oh, how it must hurt him! Oh, isn't it nuts!
Oh, what jolly sharp stinging good fleshy hard cuts!
How each lash leaves its mark well cut into the flesh!
How each cut must leave Algernon tingle afresh!
Don't it hurt your poor bottom, my boy — don't it hurt!
Don't you wish you might rub it — just once with your shirt?
Don't you wish — don't you wish you could rub it just once?
[…]
[…]
[…]
[…]
(The master stops flogging Algernon and holds the birch over his bottom

Master. Now, Algernon, what do you think of the birch?

[Algernon]. [O by …] — sir please, [leave …]
[…] the skin [off] my bottom! […]

[Master.] & sensitive part […]
Does it smart? does it smart, sir? does that [smart, sir?]
(Applying the birch most vigorously to Algernon's bottom.

Algernon. Oh!

Master. [Aye], does it smart, my boy?

Algernon. (writhing under the lash). Spare me, sir!

Master. (applying the birch to Algernon's bottom with the utmost strength of his arm). **No!**

Algernon. Oh!

Master. No crying here! does it smart, my boy?

Algernon. (roaring with the pain). Oh!

Master. No crying, I say! I'll have no crying here, sir! (Flogs him again.

Rod. Swish!

Algernon. Oh, sir!

Master. Hush! (Flogs him again.

Rod (whipping Algernon). Swish!

Algernon (screaming with pain). Oh!

Rod (whipping him again). Swish!

Algernon (looking up in the master's face with streaming eyes). Oh, sir! Oh, […] sir!

Master. Does it hurt, my boy? eh, my boy? […]

[…] […]

[…] […]

[…] […] (Flogs him again.

Rod. Swish!

Algernon. Oh!

[Master] […] feels […]
[…]
Don't you [wish,] don't you wish you could just […]
your […]
Don't you wish you [could pull] down your shirt?
don't you wish
[You could …] up, Algernon!

Rod (whipping Algernon's bottom again). Swish!

Algernon. Oh!

Rod. Swish!

Algernon (crying bitterly). Oh, sir, please let me off, sir!

Rod (whipping Algernon's bottom more and more severely). Swish!

Algernon (crying & sobbing most bitterly under the rod). Oh!

Algernon's Flogging.

Rod. Swish! (Whipping Algernon's bottom.
Algernon. Oh! (Algernon writhes with pain at each cut of the rod.
Master. Let you off again, Algernon? No!
Algernon. Oh, please, sir! I'll never be late again.
Master. (raising the birch to the utmost height possible). Pish!
Algernon. Oh, I'll never be caught out of bounds again.
Rod. (whipping his bottom again. Swish!
Leonard. Oh, I say, look at Algernon's bum as he kneels!
[…] What a jolly red bottom!
Arthur. What […]
Percy. Aye, […] to the quick when […]
Oh, it's jolly to see a big bloody bare bottom!
[…] Only look at the lashes on Algernon's bum!
Only hark to the sound of the [twigs on Algernon's …]
[…] on the bum […]
[…] […]
[…] […]
[…] […]
[…] […]
[…] […]
[…] […]
[…] […]
[…] […] the blood […]
[…] […] blushing […]
George. Hit him hard, sir! Make Algernon blubber & bellow!
No, your flogging's not half over yet, my fine fellow —
You must have such a taste of the birch from behind you,
That your bottom will smart for a month to remind you.

Master. Now, Algy, my boy, hold your bottom out — so!
(whips Algernon soundly.
Rod. Swish!
Algernon. Oh!
Rod. Swish!
Algernon. Oh!
Rod. Swish!
Algernon. Oh!
Rod. Swish!
Algernon. Oh!
Rod. Swish!
Algernon. Oh!
Rod. Swish!
Algernon. Oh!
Master. S O this [rod is a good one] to [tickle the] fish. (Boys laugh.
Algernon. Oh! (The master pauses to take breath, and whips him again.
Rod. Swish!
Algernon. Oh!
Rod. Swish!
Algernon. Oh!
Rod. Swish!
Algernon. Oh!
Rod. Swish!
Algernon. Oh!
Rod. Swish!
Algernon. Oh!
Rod. Swish!
Master. Hold your tongue! don't mind me, then, eh, you young dog, you
Then I'll flog you — O, Algy, my boy, how I'll flog you!
Algernon. Oh please sir — Oh dear sir — O pray sir — O don't —
Master. What, you won't hold your tongue, then — you won't, sir — you won't?
You defy me, then, Algernon — eh, you young [...], you?
Then I'll whip you — I'll whip you — I'll whip you — I'll whip you!
And when six [months] are [past] since the day that you got 'em
still your cuts shall tell tales of the birch on your bottom.

Algernon's Flogging.

5

Algernon. Oh please, sir! Oh do let me off, sir! Oh God, sir!
Master. I'll flog you while (swish) I can hold a birch rod, sir!
(Whipping Algernon with the utmost strength of his arm.
I'll flog you as long as my arm — swish — has strength
enough (Whipping Algernon again and again.
To flog you, sir! No — you have not had at length enough!
Roar, Algernon, roar! if your bottom feels sore,
You can roar, sir, for mercy — roar, Algernon, roar!
Does it hurt? does it sting? does it cut like a knife?
I'll flog you within just an inch of your life.
You can bear it — a great big tall strong boy like you.
Algernon. Oh, I can't — I can't bear it! Oh, spare me, sir, do!
Master. You can — you can bear it, my boy — & you must.
I'm not cruel, nor even severe — but I'm just.
We shall soon see you punctual in school & in church.
Now, Reginald, give me another new birch.
For the twigs that on this one were lately so fresh
Are all frayed & worn out — but your school-fellow's flesh
Is a little the worse too for wear & for tear,
And his bottom for once is as red as his hair.
Nay, I fancy his bottom's the redder for once.
I'll make you remember this flogging, you dunce:
I'll teach you duty to me & to God.
Go, Reginald, fetch me a supple fresh rod.
(To Algernon) You'll remember henceforward to do as your bid.
Algernon (aside). Well, I'm hanged if it hurts me as much as it did.

Though it stings like the devil — & smarts like the deuce —
yet he shan't make me cry any more — what's the use?
Next time I won't cry — & I wish, oh, I wish
I had borne the first dose of it pluckily!

New Rod. (giving Algernon's naked bottom a very severe cut). Swish! 116

Master. How now, sir? grown obstinate, eh? Are you dumb?
Can't you answer the birch when it when it speaks to your bum?

Edward. By Jove, what a lark! turning rusty, by God!
Turning sulky! but won't he just catch it! The rod
Has been three days in pickle, I know, & will sting
Like a scorpion, & cut like a knife. Such a thing
Is unheard of — the school never saw it — a fellow
At the touch of the twigs on his bottom to bellow?
And be whipped by degrees into pluck & endurance
Of pain! What a spree!

George. And what awful assurance!
O, I hope I shall now see him flogged as I wished
So often to see him — I hope he'll be swished
As he never as yet been.

Wilfred. You'll soon have your wishing.
I never did see such a jolly good swishing.

Second Rod. Swish! Swish! (whipping Algernon soundly. 118

Edward. O, by Jove, what a lark!

Wilfred. Well, I'll bet
We shall hear Master Algy sing out again yet
Sing out though at present he's as mute as a fish —
Before the head master has done with him.

Rod. (whipping Algernon's naked bottom more soundly than ever). Swish!
Swish! Swish! 121

Wilfred. We shall soon have him howling for mercy
And roaring again rather louder — eh, Percy?

Chorus. 6

[S..] 1.

George. O, by Jove, what a jolly good spree!
Algernon's flogging is something to see!
Leonard. Ah! look there! how that cut made him wince!
Punished last week, he's been sore ever since!
Arthur. Algernon's bottom & Birkenshaw's rod —
A'n't they a couple of lovers, by God!
Reginald. Lovers? the banns have been spoken in church —
Here — but young Bottom don't dote on Miss Birch.
Percy. Ah, but Miss Birch, as you call her you see,
Dotes on young Bottom — & how they agree!
Frank. Poor young Bottom! just look how he blushes!
Deeper at each of her kisses he flushes.
Edward. 'Poor young Bottom,' you say, Frank, eh?
Well you may — by the Lord, you may!
Wilfred. Rosy young Bottom & randy Miss Birch
Kiss like lovers outside the church.

[S..] 2

George. 'Rosy young Bottom' is fair & ruddy —
'Randy Miss Birch' is assiduous — & bloody.
Leonard. See! O, see! How Algernon writhes!
Look at the sweep of the birch — like a scythe's!
Arthur. Algernon's bottom must know by this —
Look! just look! — how the birch can kiss!
Reginald. Know! by Jove! It's a rite of the church!
Young Master Bottom baptised by Miss Birch!
Percy. Young Master Bottom objects, it appears —
Writhes when she kisses his cheeks, & sheds tears.
Frank. Tears at each kiss he receives are shed —
Tears that run down — & the tears look red.
Edward. Scores of good floggings he's had & forgot 'em:
Well may Miss Birch be so fond of young Bottom!
Wilfred. Poor Master Bottom! in school or in church,
Still young Bottom remembers Miss Birch.

Epode 2.

George. Isn't it jolly to see!
Leonard. Poor fellow!
Arthur. Shame! It's a shame!
Reginald. He is catching it well! oh,
Look!
Percy. How he quivers with pain!
Frank. What a spree!
Edward. He's fainting!
Wilfred. He isn't, you fool — can't you see? 124
(The master whips Algernon's bottom till the blood streams & the birch buds fly.
Algernon. Oh! Oh, sir! Oh, please, sir! Please, please, sir! Oh! Oh!
Master. No crying, sir, here! I won't have it, you know.
George. That last scream was so loud you could hear it a mile hence.
By Jove, this is jolly!
Algernon. (writhing in agony under the rod). Oh, spare me, sir!
Master. Silence!
George. What a jolly good lark! It's delicious to see!
Leonard. It's a [...]!
Arthur. And a beastly one!
Reginald. Ain't it a spree!
Percy. You're a brute!
Frank. You're a fool Master Percy — it's jolly
To look at: and Redgie's quite right.
Edward. And the jolly
Is Redgie's & yours — & tomorrow I'll thrash you.
Wilfred. And won't the same rod that whips Algernon lash you!
(The master gives Algernon's bottom a final cut.
Rod. Swish! 125
Algernon. (writhing with pain). Oh!
Master. Now get up, sir! & look at the clock:
And remember the time — & the birch — & the block.
You ought to remember them. (Algernon rises from the whipping-block in tears.
George. (watching Algernon with a smile as he draws up his breeches). Some have forgot 'em:
But Algernon won't: only look at his bottom!

Note to "Algernon's Flogging."

Algernon's first taste of the birch was on his ninth birthday, when his father began a long course of flogging by the application of nine severe cuts with a tough supple rod, followed by a single cut in memory of his first birthday, two cuts to commemorate the second, three cuts to remind him of the third, four cuts in honour of the fourth, five cuts more for the fifth, six cuts over for the sixth, seven cuts more for the seventh, & eight cuts extra for the eighth; three good cuts at parting made up the score to four dozen. How the little fellow kicked & howled, howled & kicked, kicked & howled again, it is easy to imagine; but not a cut was spared till the whole dose was duly counted out on his blushing & pouting bottom, all lined with crimson ridges & beaded with spots of blood. He had several floggings in the course of the following year; & on his tenth birthday, the same ceremony was repeated. Ten cuts were well laid on to begin with; then one cut more, two cuts over, three cuts following, then four cuts extra, five cuts, then six, then seven more, eight more, & nine severe cuts to end with, most vigorously applied to the smarting bottom which had then received no less than fifty-five smart lashes. Colonel Sinclair then gave his boy five sharp cuts over, to complete his dose of five dozen; & Algy, roaring with pain, was at length [released].

Next year the exact number of fifty-five stripes was delibe-
rately told out on Algernon's backside, & a smart addi-
tional application of seven stinging & tingling stripes
made up his birchen dose to the good sound sum
of sixty-six lashes. To this liberal allowance the
addition of a sound dozen on his twelfth birthday gave
a total of seventy-eight — which with three severe
cuts by way of grace after meat made up nine times
nine — eighty-one strokes of the birch on the bottom.
On Algy's thirteenth birthday this dose was duly repeated —
the extra three cuts & all, though the boy (if he thought
at all of it) had hoped to be let off three; but they were
wanted — as usual — to make up the account of his flagellation
in round numbers. Thirteen stripes over made ninety-four:
& the Colonel gave his bleeding boy six cuts more to make up
a hundred. On the luckless boy's fourteenth birthday
ninety-one strokes of the birch were most lustily and
vigorously applied to his naked writhing posteriors
before the day's allowances of fourteen lashes was
duly & smartly laid on; after which three cuts were
generously thrown in to complete the infliction of nine dozen.

The Flogging-Block. Eclogue II. Reginald's Flogging.

Scene — the private flogging-room.
Schoolmaster — Reginald.

Master. How often this half have I flogged you, Loraine?
Reginald. Twenty-six times, sir — please, sir, don't whip me again!
Don't flog me this once, sir! I wasn't in church,
I know — I was fagging —
Master. Boy, look at this birch;
Does it look like a tickler — a stinger?
Reginald. Oh, please, sir —
Master. Come, down with your trousers — & down on your knees, sir
You were whipped, I remember, for breaking some rule,
The very first day of your coming to school —
You remember?
Reginald. Oh yes, sir — remember it well.
Master. And you wrote to your father — complaining — to tell
The tale of your sufferings: he sent me your letter —
'You have flogged my boy well, sir, it seems: flog him better
Next time, & still better the next time: the pain
May improve him.
Yours faithfully,
Arthur Loraine.'
When I read out that letter in school — it was all
The reply that you got, or deserved — you may call
Pretty clearly to mind what a shout of derision
Went from the upper & lower division;
And I think you may probably — not without pain —
Recollect the result of it, Redgie Loraine.
Reginald. Yes, please, sir, I do — but —
Master. You whimper in vain.
Kneel down on the whipping-block, Redgie Loraine:

Reginald. Oh, please, sir! This once, sir!
Master. Go down, sir!
This once!
Reginald. Oh, do let me off, sir! This once, sir!
Master. You dunce,
Each minute you keep the rod waiting — by God,
I'm ashamed of you! — means a fresh stroke of the rod.
Go down. Algy Clavering, Fred Norton, Frank Fane,
Arthur Clifford, would blush for you, Redgie Loraine
You saw how I whipped Algy Clavering, in school
Only yesterday — how can you be such a fool
As to risk a flogging? I bid you again
Go down on the flogging-block, Redgie Loraine.
Reginald. Oh yes, sir — oh please, sir! (Reginald kneels.
Master. Your shirt's in the way
Of the strokes of the birch: take it up, sir, I say
Reginald. Oh please, sir — oh yes, sir! (takes up his shirt, and shows his naked bottom.
Master. Well, Redgie, no wonder
You've been reluctant to lift it, & show what is under.
You are nicknamed, I hear, in the lower division,
Pepperbottom — a term of appropriate derision.
Who gave you that name, sir?
Reginald. George Charlton, sir.
Master. Yes —
You're his fag: he's a rather hard master, I guess.
I never knew anyone take such delight,
When a schoolfellow has to be whipped, in the sight.
I believe — his delight is so frank & explicit —
He would rather himself have a whipping than miss it.

Well, he'll shortly be here, by express invitation,
To witness his cousin Loraine's flagellation,
With five or six others — or seven — I forgot 'em
Just now — but the sight of your great naked bottom
Reminds me what boys are invited to come
And see me unsparingly brushing your bum.
For I shan't do it sparingly, sir, you may swear; you
Can hardly, I fancy, expect me to spare you.
Reginald. Oh, don't let them all come to see me, sir! pray!
I don't mind it as much if you'll send them away.
Don't send for them — then I can bear it with ease.
Don't — don't let them all see you whipping me, please!
Master. But suppose I don't want you to bear it with ease, sir?
No, I want you to feel & remember it.
Reginald. (crying bitterly) Please, sir!
Oh, please, sir, I'll try to do better — I will —
I will, sir, indeed! — I'll be perfectly still
While you're whipping me! still as a fellow can be!
Please, flog me at once, sir, & don't let them see!
Please, whip me, sir — whip me before they come in!
Oh, take up the birch, sir, so, please, & begin!
Master. Don't you know that I won't be petitioned & pestered — eh?
You saw how I whipped your friend Algernon yesterday,
And I saw how you chuckled at sight of his pain:
Won't he chuckle at sight of your bottom, Loraine?
However, as never before such a wish
Was expressed, you shall have your petition, sir. Swish!
(Flogs Reginald.
Swish! Swish!
Reginald. (sobbing violently). Oh! Oh! Oh, sir!
Master. (flogging him again). Don't make such a noise,
Or I'll punish you, Reginald. Here come the boys.

Enter Algernon Clavering, George Charlton, Leonard Dacre,
Arthur Clifford, Percy Featherstonhaugh, Frank Fane,
Edward Collingwood, and Wilfred Reed.

Master. Come in, my lads, all; but stand out of the way:
Make room for the sweep of the birch:

Edward. (aside to Arthur). Oh, I say,
Isn't Reginald catching it? catching it hot?
Just look at the weals on his flesh! what a lot!

Master. Stand back there, George Charlton — stand back, if you wish
To see the rod tickle young Reginald. Swish!
Swish! Swish! (Flogging Reginald severely.

Reginald. (roaring with the pain). Oh! Oh! Oh!

Master. (flogging him). Hold your tongue! Hold your tongue!

Arthur. O, by Jove, I say, Ned, how that last must have stung!

Master. I'll whip you again for this crying: you had
Fair warning — I said I would whip you, my lad,
If you cried — I would whip you, & whip you again
And whip you for crying & roaring with pain:
And now you shall feel how I'll whip you, Loraine.

Reginald. (crying & sobbing). Please, please, sir! Oh! Oh! I can't bear it! I can't!

George. (aside). Yes, you'd like just to rub your backside — but you shan't.

Reginald. (crying). I can bear it no longer — indeed, I can't bear it, sir!
Oh, spare me, sir! Spare my poor bottom, sir! Spare it, sir!

George. (mimicking Reginald, aside). 'Oh, spare my poor bottom!'

Master. (flogging Reginald with all the strength of his arm). How dare you, Loraine,
Disobey me? I see I must whip you again.

Reginald. (sobbing bitterly). Oh! Oh! Oh!

Master. (flogging him). I'll have no crying here, sir!

Reginald. (choking with his tears). Augh! Augh!
Oh! Oh, sir! (Reginald pulls down his shirt and rubs his bottom.

Master. Here, Percival Featherstonhaugh,
— You're the biggest and strongest boy here as beholder
of Reginald's flogging, though Charlton is older —
Lay hold of his hands: if you once let them slip, you
Will smart for it, Percy my boy; for I'll whip you
As soon as he's risen from the whipping-block's ledge he
Now kneels on.
Percy. All right, sir: I'm stronger than Redgie.
Edward (aside). I should think you just were! why, you're stronger than George.
Leonard (aside). Redgie's bottom is burning like fire in a forge,
Poor fellow! it's easy to see by the colour
How it smarts at each stroke — and the pain won't grow duller
For hours upon hours — & the cuts won't be healed
For a week!
Wilfred (aside). O, I say, how his bottom is wealed
All over! one mass of red ridges — a study
For colourists — eh, Ned? Just look at his bloody
Bare bottom — the sunset is never as ruddy!
Arthur (aside). He won't stop till poor Redgie's all covered with blood:
It's a beastly, black shame! and each twig has a bud
At the tip! it's all rough, tough, green, supple & buddy —
What a rod! and poor Reginald's bottom all bloody!
I can't think how he bears it.
Algernon (aside). He's faint with the pain.
Master (flogging Reginald). Take that! And take that, Master Redgie Loraine!
And take that, sir — and that! And take that, sir, again!
And take that! And take that! And take that! 21 cuts
Percy (aside). What a rain
Of birch on the bottom!
Master (giving Reginald a very severe cut). Take that too, Loraine.

Reginald (writhing in agony under the torture). Oh! Oh, sir!
Master (giving him another sharp cut). Take that! and don't make such a noise!
And now, as my arm's growing weary, my boys,
You shall each one in turn take the rod, do you see?
And each shall give Redgie three cuts — only three.
And the boy that hits hardest, & gives him most pain
And makes him cry loudest for mercy in vain,
And flogs him still harder while roaring for mercy,
Shall get off his next flogging. Here — you, Master Percy,
Begin: you're the biggest boy present. (Hands him the rod.

Percy. But, please, sir,
This rod's all worn out — he could bear it with ease, sir;
It will only just titillate Reginald's rump;
It won't hurt him — to speak of, sir, — won't make him jump:
There's hardly a bud on it left: I'm afraid
It won't hurt: & all the twigs are all broken & frayed.
It won't hurt him a bit.

Master. Let me look at it. Faugh!
Quite useless! Yes, Percival Featherstonhaugh,
You're quite right: you're a sensible boy, and you've spoken
Like an honest one. Yes — all these birch twigs are broken
And worn — & the rod has got hardly a bud on it —
Though, boys, you can all see your schoolfellow's blood on it.
(Holding up the rod.
Go and fetch me another — green, sappy, & supple.
No — don't bring another birch rod; bring a couple.

Algernon (aside). By Jove this is really to bad! How I wish
I could lick that brute Charlton, who grins like a fish
At each cut! (Percy brings out two rods from a closet.

Master. Now begin, my boy.

Percy. Yes, sir. Swish! Swish!
(Flogs Reginald.

Master. Not too fast! not too fast! let him feel the full pain.
Of each cut — the full sting — the full smart of it: vain
Is the lash of the birch on the bottom that leaves
No time for the tender sore flesh that receives
The stripe to appreciate & relish the pain.

Percy. Oh yes, sir, I know. Swish! (Percy flogs Reginald.

Reginald (roaring aloud with agony). Oh!

Master. Redgie Loraine,
I'm ashamed of you: boys whose misconduct in church
And in school-time must needs bring upon them the birch
Should have courage enough to be able to bear it.
Now, Collingwood, take up the birch — & don't spare it.
(Percy hands the birch to Edward.

Edward. I won't, sir. Swish! Swish! (Flogging Reginald.

Reginald (writhing under the lash). Oh! Oh! Oh!

Master. Now, again.

Edward. One minute — just one — to take breath, sir: Loraine
Will smart all the more for it. Swish! (Edward flogs Reginald.

Reginald (crying & sobbing & wriggling his bottom about on the block). Oh! Oh! Oh!

Master. Now, Willie, my boy, it's your turn — & you know
What's meant by a flogging. (Edward hands the birch to Wilfred.

Wilfred. I do, sir, indeed.

Master. Then mind that Loraine shall remember it, Reed.
(Wilfred flogs Reginald.

Reginald (choking with half-stifled sobs) Oh! Oh!

Master. Pretty well — not so bad, my boy: still
You won't get the prize of the whipping-bout, Will —
You won't be let off your next flogging. Now, Fane,
It's your turn: take the birch, and don't spare young Loraine.
(Wilfred hands the birch to Frank.

32

George (aside). This is almost more jolly than yesterday: then
Algy Clavering was jolly well swished, too — but when
Redgie's bottom comes under my lash, we shall see!
(Frank flogs Reginald.

Master (smiling). One! — Good! very good, Frank! — Two! — Excellent! — Three!
You can hit pretty hard, I see, Frank. (Reginald sobs aloud.

Frank. Yes, sir. Thank you.

Master. For what?

Frank. O, for letting me whip him.

Master. Why, Frank, you
Haven't learnt from past sufferings the lesson of mercy:
But neither had Edward — & neither has Percy.
You have used him as dogs use his namesake, old Reynard,
When they catch him. And now let us see whether Leonard
Will beat you in beating Loraine with the birch.
He is still under sentence for whispering in church,
And tonight or tomorrow will smart for it, God
Knows — smart for it soundly, when under the rod —
Unless (in redemption, you see, of my pledge) he
Can avoid it by laying the lash upon Redgie
More soundly than others — I stick to my pledges —
And save his own bottom by punishing Redgie's.

Leonard. I'll try, sir. (Frank hands the birch to Leonard.

Master. I'm certain you will: but your maker
Didn't make you, I fancy, quite strong enough, Dacre.
(Leonard flogs Reginald.

Reginald (aside, while wincing under the lash). I won't — no, I won't cry — not this time: if any
Boy does get off next time, it shall not be Lenny.

Master. Stop, Dacre — you've had your three cuts, sir: no farther.
Give Clifford the birch. Take the birch from him, Arthur.

Arthur. I'd rather not flog him, sir, please.
Wilfred (aside to Arthur). You're a trump!
Percy (aside). What a fool!
Master. But you must, sir. (Leonard hands the birch to Arthur.
George (aside). How Reginald's rump
Will smart, after this, when it comes to my turn!
(Arthur flogs Reginald.
Master. Well done, boy! in spite of your friendly concern,
I see you know how to make any boy smart.
One! — Two! — Very good! Now draw breath, & take heart,
And give him a stinging sharp cut — if you wish
To keep clear of the whipping-block.
Arthur (laughing). Don't I, sir? Swish!
Reginald. Oh! Oh, I can't bear it!
Master. You can't? That's unlucky, boy,
For you: it would need a remarkably plucky boy
To bear what you yet have to bear, without slavering
And sniffling. Come here, Master Algernon Clavering,
If you can — if the cuts & the sores haven't festered — eh? —
That were left by the stripes which were laid on you yesterday:
And mind, if you wouldn't be punished again,
That you lay the lash well upon Redgie Loraine.
(Arthur hands the birch to Algernon.
'Ain't it a spree?' were his words — for I heard
Each whispered, subdued, inarticulate word
That ran round the group of the boys who were dogging you
With their eyes, so to speak, all the time I was flogging you.
Now punish him well for those words.
(Algernon flogs Reginald.
Master (after the first cut). What does this mean?
George (aside). Why, he's letting him off out of pity! That is mean!

Master (to Algernon). You're not hitting as hard as you can — not by half.

Algernon (laughing). O no, sir.

Master. And why, sir? And why do you laugh?

Algernon. Because, sir, I think it would be *a* damned shame.
Just look at his bottom, poor fellow! the game
Isn't fair.

Master. Ah! you swear — & defy me? Now, mind,
If you spare him again when you hit him behind,
You'll repeat it.

Algernon. I don't think I shall — but your wish
Is my law, sir. Swish!

Reginald. Oh!

Algernon. Is that better, sir? Swish!

Master. I thought you two boys were not friends: but I see 44
You are trying to spare him.

Algernon. Of course: it would be
A nice thing, sir, wouldn't it, rather, if I
Were to take it just now out of Redgie — to try
If I couldn't, by help of the birch, make him cry?
I do hope, sir, I'm not such a sneak as all that.

George (aside). You mayn't be a sneak — but O ain't you a flat!

Master. Very right, my boy — yes — very right. But Loraine
Deserves, for repeated transgressions, the pain
That you ought to have given him. However, that's past.
Now, Charlton, it's *your* turn to give him the last
Three cuts that are wanting — just three — to complete
His punishment. Here's a fresh rod. (Hands a birch to George.

George (aside). What a treat!
(aloud). But please, sir, three's nothing — I *must* give him nine!

Oh, you'll see how I'll make him sing out, sir, & whine!
Oh, do, sir, please do let me give him a dozen!

Master (smiling). Well, Charlton, Loraine is your fag, & your cousin —
You've a night to lay hands on him — do as you please.
But remember your victim is down on his knees —
And don't be too hard on him.

George (grinning.) No, sir — not I!

Master. Well, begin, then — you're keeping him waiting.

George. I'll try
If this birch is a stinger, or not — & this cut
Won't count, sir — now, will it? (George flogs Reginald.

Master. Don't stick in the rut —
Move on, sir; & give him another.

George. All right, sir. (Flogs him again.
But the birch should be buddier — & supple & light, sir. (Flogs him again.

Master. Most certainly. Bring me another, Frank Fane.

Reginald (sobbing). Oh! Oh!

George (aside to Reginald). Won't you smart when I hit you again!
And we haven't begun yet, you know, you young dog, you;
And, by Jove, when we do, you shall see how I'll flog you!

Reginald (aside to George). You're a brute — I don't care if you flog me to death,
You bully! I'll say so as long as I've breath.

Algernon (aside to Arthur). Did you hear him? I say, cousin Redgie's a plucky boy!

Arthur. Of course! but (like you) he's a [precious] unlucky boy!

(Frank hands a new birch rod to George. George flogs Reginald again

George. Take that, my boy! Swish!

Master. Take a step or two back [48]
After each cut — then bring down the birch on him — smack!
It needs the full sweep of the arm, & the weight
And the impulse it gives to the stroke — which is great —
To make the rod sting to the quick, as it should.
I'm advising you only for Reginald's good.

George. Yes! Thank you, sir! Swish! (George flogs Reginald again.
Reginald (roaring with pain). Oh! Oh! Oh!
George. You don't mind it!
Your bum doesn't know if a birch is behind it —
If a rod's hanging over it — does it, my lad?
Swish! Swish!
Algernon (aside to Wilfred). O, I say, this is getting too bad!
Wilftred. Remember the swishing your own bottom had
Only yesterday; wasn't that worse — or as bad?
Algernon. Well, of course I was jolly well swished — (Reginald screams.
How he bellows,
Poor chap! — but not whipped by a lot of you fellows.
The pain, very probably, Reed, was the same:
But — whipped by your schoolfellows! Think of the shame!
Wilfred. I don't see where the shame is; & Redgie Loraine,
I'm certain, is thinking much more of the pain.
Algernon. Well he may! How George Charlton lays into him! Oh,
By Jove, it's too bad, Willie! cruel, you know!
George (flogging Reginald). Take that, Redgie! Swish! And take that, sirrah! Swish!
And take that, cousin Reginald! Swish! How I wish
I could flog, flog, flog, flog you as much as I like!
But at least you shall feel — Swish! — how hard I can strike.
Reginald (appealing to the master). Oh, please, sir, he'll kill me! Oh! Oh!
Master. No, he won't.
George. Take that, Master Redgie! (Flogging him again.
Redgie (writhing & roaring). Oh! Charlton! Oh! Don't!
George (flogging him). Take that! What a jolly good rod it is, cousin!
Swish!
Reginald (roaring) Oh!
George (flogging him again). And take that! Swish!
Master. That makes up the dozen.

George. Oh, do, sir, please do let me give him one more!
Just one! I did hope I might give him a score,
But at least let me give him a round baker's dozen,
Do, please, sir!
Master (smiling). All right!
George (raising the birch). Now look out, my dear cousin!
For, though I mayn't give you as much as I wish,
I think I shall tickle your bum for you! **Swish!**
Reginald. Oh! — Oh!
Master. That's enough: You'll remember the pain
As long as you live to remember, Loraine;
I should hope so at least. Now get up. — Let him go.
Reginald (rising from the whipping-block). Oh! Oh! how it smarts! how it tingles! Oh! Oh!
Master (aside). Poor fellow! His conduct was certainly bad enough —
But he has had enough! Though his friends will be glad enough
To hear of it. Yes, he has certainly had enough!
Leonard. Oh, look how he's crying & writhing & trying
To button his breeches up, sobbing & sighing
And groaning & moaning with pain! What a spree!
Arthur. Well, I think it's too bad!
Percy. But it's jolly to see!
Frank. He stops at each button to rub himself; then
(Just look!) goes on buttoning & rubbing again.
Edward. As if rubbing his bottom would rub off the weals!
Wilfred. But it lessens the smart for the moment: one feels
— As the pain finds expressing in crying & sobbing —
Just a little relief from the burning & throbbing
Of the newly made weals & fresh cuts & raw stripes.
Algernon. Poor devil! I feel for him — look how he wipes
His eyes on the sleeve of his jacket, while trying
To settle his breeches & shirt, & stop crying!
Arthur. Well, I think it's too bad! And he's sure to hear chaff enough.
George. You young idiot! I tell you he hasn't had half enough!

Arthur. You'd kill him, poor fellow; I think, if you could.
What on earth makes you hate him so? Redgie's as good
And honest & plucky a boy, & as kind
And good-humoured & jolly & bright, as you'll find.
Why on earth do you spite him so?

George. Why? he disgraces us
All — all his relations at school — & outfaces us
With a plea like an idiot's whose speech is mere slavering.
'He is no worse' — & he isn't — 'than Algernon Clavering.'
I wish I could see them both whipped as they should be!

Arthur. Well, by Jove, if you haven't already, that would be
A whipping!

George. It would! How I wish that it could be!

Master. Now, Reginald, listen to me. You have had
A taste of deserved flagellation, my lad;
And you'll never be able to hold up your face again
In school, if you ever incur such disgrace again.
Such disgrace has been never inflicted on any boy
But you: it is not that the stripes were so many, boy,
Though I seldom give any boy's bottom five dozen,
But that all the boy's present have whipped you — your cousin
George Charlton especially; this, on the face of it,
Ought to make a boy blush for the shame & disgrace of it.
And I trust that the shame, if you don't mind the pain,
Or the pain, if the shame doesn't sting you, Loraine,
To the quick, as it should do, & would do, I know,
If you were not so headstrong, may work on you so
That I mayn't have to flog you again, sir — or rather —
(That's too much to expect, I'm afraid!) that your father
May not get such a shameful report of your folly — days
Upon days of disgrace! — when you're home for the holidays,
As last half you took home — that would be a disgrace for you!
And now, get to bed, my boy: bed's the best place for you.

Epilogue to Reginald's Flogging.

Scene — a small dormitory in Much Birchingham School,
Rodbury, Northumberland.

Enter Reginald Loraine, fresh from the flogging-block,
crying, and writhing with pain, and rubbing his bottom;
followed by Arthur Clifford, shrugging his shoulders and laughing.

Reginald (sobbing bitterly). Oh, I say, they've half killed me!
Arthur. Don't rub the sore parts so:
You'll make your sores worse.
Reginald. Oh, but, Arthur, it smarts so!
It burns so! it burns like the fire in a forge!
I can't bear it!
Arthur. You have been well punished, by George!
Reginald. By George! Don't I wish I could lick him, the beast!
Arthur. Well, you've had enough — and as good as a feast.
Reginald. A feast! Don't I wish that brute Charlton could share it!
Arthur. Well, Loraine, you must grin — or must blubber — & bear it.
It's useless, you know, writing home to complain —
As you know by experience. Eh? don't you, Loraine?
Reginald (angrily). Oh, of course you can chaff me — you know you can chaff
Just now —
Arthur. Why, Loraine, any fellow would laugh
To look at you writhing & crying so — blubbing
Like a girl — & then rubbing & rubbing & rubbing
Your unfortunate bottom! I say, my boy, come,
Be a man; though the birch-twigs have tickled your bum
Pretty smartly, they haven't 'half killed you': that's rot:
It's mere whining & whimpering, — you know they have not.

Reginald. Ah, it's all very well — & good-natured — your pitching
Into me: how do <u>you</u> like a jolly switching?
I remember, last time you & Birkenshaw differed,
How you roared on the flogging-block: didn't you, Clifford?
And you didn't get half such a flogging — not half —
As I've had. It's cheeky, I must say, to chaff,
When you know that you couldn't stand half what I've stood.

Arthur. You stand it? By Jove, Master Redgie, that's good!
Why, you know you were crying & screaming & roaring
The whole time — & the tears were incessantly pouring,
Down your cheeks — I don't wonder — I don't say I do:
But don't talk about standing it, Redgie. Not you!

Reginald (trying not to cry again). It's good-natured, I must say — good-natured & plucky —
To bully a fellow who's always unlucky.
Your governor doesn't write letters — I wish you
Had a father like mine! — asking people to swish you
(As if he was likely to spare me, by God!) —
'Flog Reginald well, sir — don't grudge him the rod!'
He says he don't mind — never did — never will —
How much money for birch is put down in the bill
For each half — & he reads it all out — & he chaffs —
'You'll cost me a fortune in birch, boy!' — & laughs.

Arthur. Poor old Redgie! By Jove, what a shame! But you do
Wear a good lot of birch out each half: that is true.
And you shouldn't fall blubbering & snivelling & slavering
When your birched, man.

Reginald. (indignantly). I don't!

Arthur. But you do! Look at Clavering.
Algy Clavering, I mean — not young Charlie, of course —
When he's horsed, with that brute of a porter for horse,
Don't you see how he takes it, Loraine, without flinching —
Just frowning with pain at each cut, & just pinching
His lips up together, & clenching his fists
When the fellow who's horsing him pinches his wrists?

Reginald. Well, but yesterday, Clifford, you know, after Church,
How he roared at the very first touch of the birch —
At the very first taste of the twigs on his bum —
And you know how you mocked him.
Arthur. Come, come, Redgie, come —
I know how he blubbered — and bellowed — at first —
And the swishing he got was the worst — quite the worst
That ever I saw a boy get: but, my friend,
Forget the beginning — remember the end!
He managed to swallow his sobs, & to stifle
His cries — & the flogging he got was not trifle!
I never saw quite such a whipping as that.
Reginald. It's like your ill-nature — I see what you're at —
You want to make out (don't come pinching & nipping me!)
That I wasn't worse off — not with nine fellows whipping me —
And whipping as though they would never have done
(And I half thought they wouldn't't) — than Algy with me.
Arthur. Well, I don't think you were: though we gave you some pain,
(It *was* rather hard on you, really, Loraine)
George Charlton himself (how he made your tears flow!)
Can't hit quite so hard as the Doctor, you know.
But — as gardeners dig weeds in the gardens with spuds out —
Don't you want me to help you to pick the birch buds out?
Your bottom's stuck full of them. (Aside). Won't he just yelp!
Reginald. Don't hurt me, please, more than you really can help.
Arthur. Well, I won't — on my honour. But mind you don't bellow
With the pain — & I'll try not to hurt you, old fellow.
Come, take down your breeches, & take up your shirt:
Let me see your whipped bottom. Of course it will hurt:
Reginald (smiling). Of course: as to that no two boys ever differed.
But you wouldn't take pleasure in hurting me, Clifford?
I couldn't take pleasure in giving you pain.
Arthur. No, Redgie — I won't. On my honour, Loraine.
(Reginald unbuttons his trousers, lets them fall, lies
down across his bed, & lifts up his shirt behind.
By Jove, poor old lad, what a flogging you've had!

And I gave you three of those cuts, my poor lad.

Reginald. Yes, you did — but you didn't hit hard till the third;
That was kind of you, Arthur — it was.

Arthur. On my word,
You're a jolly good fellow, Loraine; any other
Would spite me.

Reginald. (laughing). O, if you'd been whipping your brother,
You wouldn't have whipped him more gently — of course,
It did sting — it did hurt — but it might have been worse:
And I didn't half mind it, old chap — not a button —
I didn't indeed — till you laid the third cut on.
That did hurt! But it wasn't your fault, you know.

Arthur. True —
All the same, it's most jolly & plucky of you
To say so. I know — and I won't say I guess —
I must really have hurt you most awfully.

Reginald. Yes;
You did, when you hit me the third time. But, come,
Don't let's talk of it, Arthur: these buds in my bum
Do hurt me so!

Arthur. Yes, I should think they just did!
Some are stuck in the flesh, man, so deeply, they're hid
In it, all but the tip of the twig; & to draw it
Right out — O, it will make you howl, man! I saw it
Was pain hardly bearable yesterday, when
I performed the same office for Algernon: then
He did writhe! there were dozens of buds in his rump.

Reginald. But, I say, isn't Algernon Clavering a trump!
I thought he would spite me — I did think he would —
I was sure he would hit me as hard as he could —
And he didn't! & wouldn't, though Birkenshaw said
'Whip him harder!' & threatened to whip him instead.
I do call that pluck, & goodnature! And I,
Only yesterday laughed when the birch made him cry!

And he spared me today, when you all whipped me well — O,
He's a brick!

Arthur. Yes, old Algy's not half a bad fellow.
What on earth made you think he would spite you, you fool?
I don't fancy he spites any boy in the school —
Though the Doctor spites <u>him</u>. And why should he?

Reginald. You see,
He's my cousin.

Arthur. What then?

Reginald. And so's Charlton — & he
Does spite me!

Arthur. He certainly does, my poor boy;
He was grinning & wriggling & chuckling with joy
All the time you were flogged, till it came to his turn
To make this bare bum of yours tingle & burn:
But all that only proves what no boy would dispute —
Algy Clavering's a brick, & George Charlton's a brute.

Reginald. But, I say, what a shame it is, Arthur, you know,
That George should get off & that Algernon — O,
It's too bad! — should be flogged three or four times a week
— Three or four times at least — while that bully and sneak
(It would make a chap cry — but it makes a chap laugh!)
Gets only one or two swishings each half.

Arthur. Ay, Redgie — I'll bet you that Algernon's father
Is like yours, & believes in the birch, & would rather
Have him flogged — ay, & well flogged — than not:

Reginald. Yes, I know he would
See Birkenshaw bumbrushing Algernon — O, he would!
— Each morning in school, & each evening again
After school in the flogging-room, gladly; & then,
When at bedtime he saw poor old Algernon stripping
For bed, he would give him another good whipping.

Arthur. See Birkenshaw bumbrushing Algernon, eh?
By Jove, if he'd only come here then, & stay
Just a fortnight, he'd surely — & then he'd have fine times! —
See Birkenshaw bumbrushing Algernon nine times.
No fellow gets bumbrushed, if that's what you call it,
So often as Algy — not one of us all — it
Seems part of the days of the week — at least, of each other
Day's work; to see Clavering well swished. — Is your mother
His aunt, then?

Reginald. Yes: Algy's & George's & mine
Were sisters. But, Clifford, — I'll try not to whine
Or squeak or sing out — won't you do as you said
You would? I do want so to get into bed!

Arthur. All right! but your bottom's one mass of red weals
And cuts & sore places — I know how it feels! —
I'll try, though. Here goes for the first great green bud
Of birch, on the right side of your bottom! the blood
Will follow —

Reginald (writhing). Oh! Arthur! Oh! Oh!

Arthur. What the deuce —
Don't you know it must hurt you, Loraine? — is the use
Of asking a fellow to pick the buds out
Of your bottom, & then setting up such a shout?

Reginald. I'm awfully sorry.

Arthur. You ought to be! Come —
There are twenty more pieces of birch in your bum;
Do you want them picked out, Master Redgie, or don't you?

Reginald. Yes — yes. But you'll try not to hurt me so — won't you?

Arthur. I can't answer at all for not hurting you, man,
But I promise I'll hurt you no more than I can.

Another Epilogue.

Spoken by an old Etonian, the Head Master's guest & contemporary, who has witnessed Reginald's double swishing & has followed him out of the flogging-room to have a word or two with the sufferer — & by Reginald in reply.

O. E   You've had it pretty hot, my boy: it beats
        All I remember when the rod was Keate's.
Regi.   Why, didn't Keate give more than that, sir, ever?
O. E.   (laughing) He never gave so much as you've had — never.
        However grave might be the fault or folly.
        He never gave so much, sir.
Regi.   Oh, — that's jolly.
O. E.   At least, he may have given as many cuts, Regi. Oh, — that's jolly.
        But not so many quite so hard. That's 'nuts' (Word for word
        For you to hear, my boy: I do not guess, from life.
        I know you're glad to hear it — a'n't you?
Regi.   Yes.
        Please, were you often swished, sir?
O. E.   Twice a week,
                          ~~can Hawtrey~~
        At least. ~~You wonder how he deigns to speak~~
        ~~To me~~ But you just beat us all for cheek.
        How long have you been here, to dare to chaff
        The birch & block?
Regi.   Two years, sir, & a half.

O. E. How old are you, my lad?

Regi. Fourteen today, sir.

O. E. A birthday you'll remember always — eh sir?

Regi. Well, I don't know, sir, quite — perhaps I may, sir.

O. E. Why, did you ever get before, my lad,
Quite so severe a whipping as you've had
This morning? Then your record must be bad!

Regi. I've had a double swishing, if you mean
That — with two birches, & the cuts fourteen —
Six times before, I think, [1) A fact] to tell the truth.
I'm not quite sure.

O. E. Well, you're a hopeful youth!
Where are you going now?

Regi. To Cuckoo Weir, sir.

O. E. Your schoolfellows will laugh to see you there, sir,
Stripped for a swim: tho? on the river shore
You'll show them, I don't doubt it, little more
Than most of them have often seen before.

Regi. Well, hardly often, sir, you know. Sometimes.

O. E. You're not ashamed, of course, of all your crimes.

Regi. I'm not ashamed of getting swished, sir — who,
At Eton, is, or ever was? Were you?

O. E. Well, no.

Regi. I thought you weren't — indeed, I knew.
Good morning, sir.

O. E. Goodbye. I wish you joy. (Exit Reginald.

Reginald's Flogging.

Then Reginald no longer durst appeal,
But reddening to the roots of his red hair
For shame that cut him to the quick like steel
And stung him like a birch, but otherwhere,
Began for flagellation to prepare.
Each boy there seated in his separate station
Full soon beheld his brawny bottom bare
With broad white cheeks spread out for castigation
All scored across with signs of former flagellation.
His recent sores had just begun to heal,
But every eye that looked his bottom o'er
Saw many & many & many a bloody weal
And many & many a red ridge raised before
By many & many a stripe that left it sore
From many & many a birch worn out in vain
On Redgie's bare posteriors, bared once more
To feel once more the red rod plied amain
And writhe & smart & burn & tingle with the pain.

The Flogging-Block. Eclogue III. Percy's Flogging.

Scene — the public flogging-room.
Schoolmaster. Algernon. George. Leonard. Arthur. Reginald. Frank.
Edward. Wilfred.

Master. Where's Percival Featherstonhaugh?
(Silence.)
Worse & worse! He
Grows shameless.
Algernon (aside to Frank). I say, where the devil is Percy?
Frank. He's larking, I'll bet, up the water-side somewhere.
Algernon. And the birch will be soon playing tunes on his bum — where
It has played the same anthem so often. By God!
One would think Master Percy was fond of the rod.
Enter Percy, hot & flushed & out of breath.
Master. Good morning! And where have you been, my good lad?
Out of bounds, I don't question. However, I'm glad
To see you at last — as I missed you in church:
For I've something to say to you; so has the birch.
Percy. O, I didn't, sir, — please, — know the time — I can't help
If I'm late, sir —
Master. Oh! Can't you, indeed, you young whelp?
And I cannot possibly, Featherstonhaugh,
Help flogging you, Down with your breeches.
Percy. Oh!
Master. Pshaw!
Don't cry out, sir, before you are hurt. Strip at once;
And you soon shall have plenty to cry for, you dunce.

Percy (still panting with breath). O, I made — all the haste — that I could, sir.

Master. Ay! Did you?
— To get back, I suppose, from the parts I forbid you
To visit — the dangerous parts of the river?
But I'll teach you to fear them — to tumble and shiver
At the thought of the pool, with the birch-trees about it,
At the foot of the waterfall. There, I don't doubt it,
You've been bathing — & might have been drowned. Now, the law
Of the school is precise — & the proof's without flaw,
Take your trousers down instantly, Featherstonhaugh.

Percy. But, please, where's the proof, sir — if nobody saw?

Master. You impudent, insolent, daring young dog!
(Boxing Percy's ears.
It's a pleasure as well as a duty to flog
Such young rascals! Yes, yes, you impertinent dog, you,
(Giving him another box on the ears.
It's a pleasure as well as a duty to flog you!
And I'll flog you, you hulking young rebel and dunce, —
Young Goliath, — young Samson, — I'll flog you at once.
I'll flog you — I'll flog you, my boy, without mercy.
Take your trousers down instantly, — instantly, Percy.
(Percy lets down his trousers.

George (aside to Wilfred). There's the biggest & the brawniest backside in the school
Naked. By Jove, isn't Percy a fool!
At his age, to get whipped like a junior boy — stripped
In sight of us all — kneeling down to be whipped.
(Percy kneels down.
Why the flogging-block really might blush, if it could,
To bear such a hulking big chap — only wood
Doesn't blush.

Wilfred. Are the birch-twigs not wood, that will blush
So soon with the blood of the bottom they brush?

George. That's true — I forgot — you remember it still —
And you've jolly good cause to remember it, Will.
Wilfred (instinctively rubbing his bottom). By Jove, I should think I just had! But, I say,
What on earth is old Birkenshaw waiting for — eh?
George. Well, not (you may swear) out of pity or mercy
Or reluctance to flog, through compassion for Percy.
Wilfred. What a great fleshy bottom — both fleshy & brawny —
As plump as two peaches — not skinny & tawny
Like yours, you know, Charlton — is Featherstonhaugh's!
What a field for the birch! And it's marked as with claws
Of wild cats — cats-o'-nine-tails, at least — here & there;
On the right side, especially, isn't it? Where
The birch has cut pieces right out of him.
George. Yes:
And it's easy — O, isn't it, Willie! — to guess
That Birkenshaw (look at him!) means, — not a doubt of him! —
At each cut that he gives him, to cut pieces out of him.
Master. Reed, bring me rod — & a cutting one, mind;
The right one to tickle a big boy behind.
(Wilfred brings him a rod.
No — this has been used: some one's bottom already
Has tasted of this: was it your bottom, Teddy?
Edward. Yes, please, sir — you flogged me last night, sir, you know.
Master. So I did. Very well, Edward Collingwood; go
And bring me a rod that will hurt — that will sting:
You should know by experience what sort of thing
Such a rod is. (Edward hands him a rod.
Yes — this has been really well soaked
In brine; & the boy whose misdeeds have provoked
Its attentions will find that it shows him no mercy.
Here, look at it, — look at the buds on it, Percy.

Compare it with that which has recently tickled
Ted Collingwood's bottom — how thoroughly pickled,
How supple, how soaked from the brine-tub all through,
Are the birch-twigs reserved, Master Percy, for you!
And I fancy (to judge by the looks of him, partly)
That I tickled Ted Collingwood's bum pretty smartly.
These twigs are all broken: there's hardly a bud left:
And I see on the tips some of Collingwood's blood left.
These reddish dry stains, & the bark that is peeled
Right off, would suggest that the parts now concealed
By his breeches must really be pretty well wealed —
Eh, Teddy?

Edward (sullenly). Well, yes, sir.

Master. Don't answer me, Ted,
So sulkily — else your posteriors, that bled
Only yesterday, may, though they must be red,
Be still redder this evening.

George (aside). I hope they'll be raw!

Master (with uplifted rod). Now, listen to me, Percy Featherstonhaugh,
This, I think, is the fortieth or, say, forty-first time
That I've whipped you this half: you'll find it the worst time
Though all present so often have seen your bum stripped, yet
I shall whip you today as you've never been whipped yet.
I shall whip you for once as you ought to be whipped
Each time your great brawny big bottom is stripped.
I shall whip you as well as your father would wish:
I shall whip you as soundly as Algernon. Swish! (Whips Percy.

George (rubbing his hands). By Jove, what a jolly good cut! What a stinger!

Wilfred. And Featherstonhaugh doesn't move — not a finger.

Leonard. He takes a good swishing that can't be avoided
As a big fellow ought.

Algernon. Ay, if ever a boy did!
He's a trump, is old Percy: it cuts to the quick,
You can see, but he bears it each time like a brick.

George. Though we all of us often have seen his bum stripped, yet
We shall now see him whipped as he's never been whipped yet:
So Birkenshaw said: & it looks like it, too!

Master. Take that, sir! (whipping Percy) We'll see if I cannot subdue
Even such a tall — stout — big — bold youngster as you
By the help of the birch. All that flogging can do
Shall be done for you, Percy: & when you've gone through
Your flogging, in sight of your schoolfellows here,
You great, big, stout, impudent young mutineer!
You shall say if a truant has nothing to fear
From the birch — if you like or don't like me to flog you,
You bold, idle, shameless, great hulking young dog, you!
(Whipping Percy severely, with a cut at each epithet
Throughout this speech, and a pause after every cut.[18]

Reginald. Not a word from him yet — not a whimper for mercy.
Oh, I wish I could stand a good swishing like Percy!

Arthur. Well, when you're as big, & have worn out as many
Birch rods, I don't doubt you will, Redgie — if any
Boy does, & is likely to smart as much, too,
And as often as Percy, I'll bet you it's you.

Master. Redgie, bring me a rod — & the buds must be green,
And the twigs must be supple & sappy — I mean
To make Percival smart — this dose of eighteen
Is nothing — as, Featherstonhaugh, you may guess, sir —
To what is coming, Loraine, do you hear me, sir?

Reginald. Yes, sir.

(Reginald brings the master a fresh, green, sappy rod.

Master (rod in had). Now, Percival Featherstonhaugh, let me tell you,
If you think you've already been whipped pretty well, you
Don't know — don't imagine — don't guess what's in store for you.
There are five rods to come, sir, — & ninety cuts more for you.

Percy (with an involuntary cry). Oh! Please, sir!

Master (laughing). I thought so — I knew 'twould be so!
Take that as a foretaste: & that, my lad! (Whips him soundly.

Percy (with a stifled sob). Oh!

Master. And remember, my lad, — eighty-eight cuts to come!
Here's the first of them, Percy. (Whips him again.

Frank (aside to Leonard). Oh, look at his bum! 21
What red ridges! What weals! What sore places! What great cuts!
He'll be flayed — flayed alive — if he gets eighty-eight cuts
More, won't he?

Master (flogging Percy severely). Take that, sir!

Percy (sobbing aloud). Oh! — Oh!

Master. Do you moan?
If you move — if you stir, boy — I'll cut to the bone.
Swish! Swish! Swish! (Flogging him very severely.

Percy Roaring with pain). Oh! Oh! Oh, sir! 24

Master (flogging him with redoubled severity). Don't howl, sir — don't groan, sir
Or I'll cut your great brawny backside to the bone, sir.
(Flogs him again. 26

Percy (roaring louder than before with agony). Oh! Oh, sir! Oh! Oh, Sir!
Master (whipping him still more severely). Take that, Mr. Percy! 27
Swish! Swish! Swish! You deserve — I'll show you — no mercy.
Did you wish — Swish! Swish! Swish! — to be able to boast 30
That of all boys I've whipped you'd been punished the most?
It would seem so — & if so, I'll give you your wish.
Swish! Swish! Swish! Swish! Swish! Swish! Swish! Swish!
Swish! Swish! Swish! Swish! Swish! 45
Percy (roaring louder than ever). Oh! Oh, sir! Oh! Oh, sir!
Leonard (aside). By Jove, what a lark!
Frank. Yes; the birch has by this time set Birkenshaw's mark
On Percy's posteriors so broadly & plainly,
If he tries to disguise it weeks hence, he'll try vainly.
Master (whipping Percy with all the strength of his arm at each Cut). Take that, Master Featherstonhaugh! You don't like it — eh?
Your bottom feels pain when it feels the rod strike it — eh?
Percy (crying & roaring with the pain). Oh, please let me off, sir! Do, please, sir! Oh!
Master (whipping him with all his might). Pshaw!
Take that! And that, Master Featherstonhaugh! 50
And take that! — And take that! — And take that! And take that!
(Whipping Percy with all the strength of his arm at each cut. 54
You young rascal! you ought to be whipped with a cat
Like the big boys in gaols: but I'll give your fill
Of the birch, — of the birch, Mr. Percy! I will! (Flogging him.
Percy (roaring & screaming with the pain). Oh, please, sir, have mercy! —
Have mercy! — Have mercy! 57

Have mercy, sir! — Spare me, sir!

Master (whipping him again). No, Master Percy. (60 cuts

The only true mercy to fellows like you
Is to whip them, & whip them again — as I do.
The one thing I can do for a boy who does ill
Is to whip him, — to whip him! And whip you I will!

(Whips Percy so severely as to draw a little stream of blood at each cut.

You should know that it's useless appealing for mercy; [63]
You must have your nine dozen, you know, Mr. Percy.
I'll teach you to shrink from the ways you should shun, — dread
Temptation.

Percy (sobbing bitterly). I'm sure I've had more than a hundred
Already — Oh, please, let me off, sir! do! do!

Master (smiling). Well, one thing is certain — & comforting, too;
That I've taken the cheek pretty well out of you,
Mr. Percy. No small boy when howling for mercy
Under punishment, ever howled louder than Percy —
No fag, ever beaten for breaking the law
Howled louder or longer than Featherstonhaugh.
The biggest boy beaten — the cock of the school,
When punished — the tallest — & the sturdiest young fool,
When whipped, as he ought to be, soundly — gives in,
You perceive, boys, & thinks but of saving his skin;
Howls, blubbers, implores, whines, & whimpers for mercy,
And vainly. — Take that! — And take that, Mr. Percy!

(Flogging Percy again with all the strength of his arm at each cut.

Percy (roaring & screaming with the pain at each cut). Oh!
Oh! Oh, sir! Have mercy! Have mercy, sir! Mercy!
I can't bear it! can't bear it! can't bear it! 72 cuts

Master (whipping Percy with the very utmost strength of his arm). Why, Percy,
I'm ashamed of you! you who should set your inferiors
An example, to cry for your smarting posteriors!
To cry like a child for your great bloody bum!
Bring some fresh rods — look sharp, Master Algernon — come
(Algernon brings the Master three or four rods to choose from.
Let me see — this is cutting — & pliant — & tough —
And the buds are quite green — & the wigs are quite rough.
I think this will do for the present. Now, Percy,
Let me hear no more crying & howling for mercy:
I advise you. (whips Percy again with all his might.

Algernon (aside to Frank). By Jove! Percy's bearing it pluckily!

Frank. You & he always do in the long run — but, luckily
For the fellows who come to look on for a spree,
You begin & you end with a howl — so does he.

Algernon. You confounded young impudent hound. What a lie!
Won't I lick you for that!

Frank. Won't you smart for it!

Algernon. I?

Frank. Yes, you, Master Algy — you'd better not try!
Don't you know that old Birkenshaw's waiting & wishing
For a pretext to give you another good swishing?

Algernon. I don't care if he is. But, I say, don't you see
He's too tired to go on whipping Percy?

Frank. Not he!

You — you, of all fellows — ought surely to know
Rather better: he's just taking breath again. (The master flogs Percy severely.

Percy (roaring louder than ever). Oh!
Oh! Oh!

Master (holding the birch suspended over Percy's naked bottom).
Now, my boys, you may see what a fool,
What a blockhead & dunce is the cock of the school
He can lick any one of you — lick you all round
So I'm told; but you hear how he roars: & the sound
Of his cries, & the sight of his bottom, should be
A warning to others whose model was he —
An example to youngsters whose dream & whose wish
Was to rival or imitate Percival. Swish!
(Flogs Percy again most soundly.

Percy (roaring afresh with pain at each cut of the birch).
Spare, spare me, Sir! — Spare me, Sir! — Spare me, Sir! — Oh!
I can bear it no longer, Sir! — Spare me, Sir!

Master (applying the birch most vigorously to Percy's bottom). No!

Percy (sobbing & panting & gasping for breath after every cut of the birch).
Spare — spare me! Oh! Oh! I can't bear it, Sir! Don't,
Don't, please, Sir don't whip me to death, Sir! I won't,
I won't, Sir, be late — or play truant, Sir! Don't,
Don't flog me so cruelly! Spare me!

Master (again applying the birch most vigorously to Percy's bottom). I won't!
I won't whip you to death — but I'll give you your share, you
Young rascal, of flogging — I'll make you take care, you
Young rogue; & I'll try how much birch you can bear, you
Young villain! — no, Featherstonhaugh, I'll not spare you!

Algernon (aside to Wilfred). By Jove, he'll half kill him — he shows him no mercy.
Well, I'm glad it's not me — but I'm sorry it's Percy.

Percy's Flogging. 6

Master (applying the birch most vigorously to Percy's naked bottom). There!
Percy (crying). Oh, Sir! 96
Wilfred (aside to Algernon). But isn't it jolly to see!
I agree with you, Algy — I'm glad it's not me.
Master (applying the birch most vigorously to Percy's naked bottom). There!
Percy. Oh!
Master. Now, before a fresh rod is applied,
As it shortly will be, to your naked backside,
(And I trust it may teach you obedience to law)
I must have a few words with you, Featherstonhaugh.
You must not suppose, if I show you no mercy,
That I take any pleasure in whipping you, Percy.
I would rather by far let you off, my boy — rather
By far — but the duty I owe to your father,
And yourself, & your schoolfellows, Featherstonhaugh,
Compels me to punish you.
Percy (crying and writhing). Spare me, sir!
Master. Pshaw!
You won't [move] me by trying to melt me or scare me
With your cries of — 'Oh, spare me, Sir! Spare me, Sir! Spare me!'
It's disgraceful! It's shameful, my lad — it's absurd!
Your behaviour is such as no father [could bear] — you
Persist in it, Percy — & ask me to spare you!
Why, when have you ever deserved that I should
Let you off, sir, one cut of the birch — if I would?
And I am not inclined, I can tell you, to mercy
In the care of a rascal like you, Mr. Percy!

And mark, me, my boy, there's a dozen to come still.

Algernon (aside to Wilfred). Just look how he wriggles — he can't keep his bum still!

Wilfred. No wonder! the sting & the scorch & the smart
Of each cut on that tender red naked sore part
Must be torture — no wonder he can't keep his bum still!
Poor Percy!

Master (whipping Percy very severely). Take that! — You've eleven to come still.
Take that! (whipping him again) and take that!
(Whipping him again.

Edward (aside to Reginald). Oh, just look at his bum!
And, Redgie, just think — there are nine cuts to come!
A'n't you glad?

Reginald. Not a bit; & why should I be, [Ned]?

Edward. Why, you know how he whipped your bare bum till it bled
At each cut, Master Redgie — & asked for a fresh
Green buddy stout birch to lay on with: your [flesh]
Must tingle & smart to remember it: so
I should think you must relish his punishment.

Reginald. No —
It was rather a shame; but I can't say I wish
To see him half killed, Ned.

Master (flogging Percy very severely indeed). Take that, my boy! Swish!
And take that — & I wish that the birch was a cat!
(Flogging harder at each cut.
And take that, Master Featherstonhaugh — & take that!

Percy (screaming & sobbing alternately after every cut). Oh, please, Sir!

Edward. By Jove, what a hard, stinging blow!

Master. (whipping Percy again & again). There, Percy — take that, my boy!

Percy (writhing with pain). Please, sir! Oh! Oh!

Master (whipping him very severely indeed). Don't writhe so — don't cry & don't jump like a fish!
Take that! — One more cut, now, at parting, sir — **Swish!**

Percy (roaring with pain, as he rises from the whipping-block). Oh! Oh! Oh!

Master (laying down the rod). Stop that crying — you're not with your [nursie]!
And button your trousers up instantly, Percy.

The Flogging-Block. Eclogue IV. Willie's Flogging.

Prelude to Willie's Flogging.

Scene, the upper schoolroom in Much Birchingham School.
Dr. Birkenshaw seated at his desk: the upper class on a
Couple of forms before him: Wilfred Reed at the bottom of the class.

Master. Reed, construe. (Willie stands up.
Begin, sir: why don't you begin?
Willie. 'Super alta —'
Edward (aside). Now, Willie, look out for your skin!
Break down once again, & you know what your fate is.
Willie. 'Across the high hills' — 'vectus Atys,' 'vexed Atys' —
'Celeri rate,' 'went at a quick rate' —
Master. Go on. My word!
What is 'maria'?
Willie. The masculine gender.
Master. Upon my word!
Have you looked at this lesson? But no; if you had,
You would be what you are not — an idiot, my lad.
Willie. I forgot what o'clock it was, please, sir; indeed —
Didn't know what the time was.
Master. Sit down, Willie Reed.
And as soon as we go out of school, my lad, come
To the birching-room.
Edward (aside). Willie, look out for your bum!
Willie. Oh, please, sir, don't whip me! Don't whip me again!
Master. Sit down while you can, Willie. Construe, Loraine.
(Reginald stands up to construe, and the scene closes.

Willie's Flogging.

Time, noon. Scene, the public flogging-room. Enter Dr. Birkenshaw, holding Willie by the collar, the other boys following in procession.

Master.	Now, take down you trousers at once, Willie.
Willie	(in an imploring voice). Please, sir!
Master.	Take them down, if you can, for him, Charlton.
George.	With ease, sir.
	(George unbuttons Willie's trousers.
Master	(to Willie). Go down on the whipping-block — down on your knees, sir.
	(Willie kneels down on the whipping-block.
	Now I'll trouble you, Charlton, to hold up his shirt.
George.	With pleasure, sir. (George pulls up Willie's shirt, and exposes his bottom.
Master.	Tell me, Will, didn't it hurt
	The last time I whipped you?
Willie.	Oh yes, sir — oh yes!
Master.	Then why — for I cannot at all, my boy, guess —
	Do I see you again on the whipping-block? Why
	Do you force me to flog you?
Willie.	Oh, please, sir, I'll try
	To do better — I'll try, sir — I will, sir, indeed.
Master.	You said so the last time I punished you, Reed.
	I shan't listen now any more, sir, than then,
	Though I'm sorry — yes, sorry to flog you again.
	You wish to do better, you say: if the wish
	Were sincere, you'd be safe from the whipping-block. **Swish!**
	(Whips Willie.
George.	There's a pretty sharp cut to begin with! Eh, Willie?
	(Aside to Willie.
Master.	Take that. You must take it, my boy, willy-nilly.
	(Whips Willie.

Willie's Flogging.

Willie (sobbing) Oh, sir!
Master. Does it hurt? (whipping Willie) does it hurt you, my lad?
I'm glad that you feel it (whipping Willie again) — I'm heartily glad.
It will help you, I trust, (whipping Willie again) if you're not quite a fool, [5 cuts]
To behave rather better in church & in school. (Whips Willie severely.
For in school you're a dunce (whipping Willie again) as you know, — & in church [6]
(Whipping Willie severely) You know how your sleepiness merits the birch. [7]
Willie (crying bitterly). Oh, please, I'm so sorry, sir! [8]
Master (whipping him again). Yes, Master Willie; [9]
I'm certain you are — don't you think you were silly
To give way to your laziness, Willie, in church? (Whips Willie.
You knew it must end in a taste of the birch, (Whips Willie soundly. [10]
Such a taste of the birch as you never yet had — [11]
Such a taste of the birch as you're getting, my lad! (Whips Willie again. [12]
Willie (sobbing). Oh! Oh!
Master. Ah! it hurts? (whipping Willie) Ah! it hurts you, my lad?
I'm glad that you smart so (whipping Willie again) — I see, & I'm glad. [13]
I see how it hurts you (whipping Willie again) — I trust you'll take warning, [14]
And be better prepared with your tasks in the morning. (Whips Willie severely. [15]
Your construing is simply disgraceful (whipping Willie again) — in church [16]
(Whipping Willie severely) Your behaviour deserves something worse than the birch [17]
Willie (crying bitterly). O, I'll try to do better, — I will, sir! [18]
Master (whipping him again). And I, [19]
Who have charge of you here, Master Willie, will try
To make sure that you shall do much better, — in church (Whips Willie.
And in school — or it shan't be for lack of the birch. (Whips Willie soundly. [20]
Had you ever, sir, — tell me, — I doubt if you had — (Whipping Willie at each pause. [21]
Such a taste of the birch — such a whipping, my lad? (Whips Willie again. [24]
Willie (crying & sobbing with pain). Oh no, sir! — Oh, never, sir — never, sir — no!
Oh, I'll never shirk school, sir, or church, again — Oh! [25]

Master (with birch uplifted). Are you sure of it, Willie? quite sure that you won't?
Willie (looking up in the Master's face — his eyes streaming with tears). Oh, yes, sir!
Master (giving Willie a sharp cut of the birch). I'm not, though, my boy.
Willie (wincing from the lash). Oh! Oh, don't!
Don't, please, sir!
Master (giving Willie another and a very severe cut). Take that, my boy.
Willie Roaring under the rod). Please, sir!
Master (laying the lash on Willie's bottom with all his strength). Take that, too!
The birch, you young rascal, shall flog such a tattoo
On your bottom as never was played on a drum.
George (aside). Oh, by Jove, a'n't it jolly to see Willie's bum!
How the birch makes it wince! — How each cut makes it bleed!
I do love to see Birkenshaw whip Willie Reed!
How he does lay the lash on! By Jove, ain't it nuts!
Master Wilfred, I'll bet, will remember these cuts
For a fortnight or more. Oh, by Jove — and all the deities
Whose sceptres or rods are of birch, what a spree it is
For all of us to see Birkenshaw tanning his hide!
How the birch seems to love Master Wilfred's backside!
How it kisses & clasps & embraces it! Then
Swings up, swishes down, & salutes it again!
How the birch-twigs bind round at each fresh cut afresh,
And leave their fresh prints on the smarting boy's flesh!
How he winces each time that the birch cuts the air,
And writhes as it cuts his bare bottom! Look there!
(The Master whips Willie more & more severely.

Willie (crying more bitterly than before). Oh! Oh, sir! — Oh! Oh!
George (chuckling — aside). How that lash must have hurt!
Has had, I should calculate, just about thirty —
Thirty stingers, too! Won't he just fidget in church!
Thirty jolly good tingling sharp cuts of the birch!
Master (whipping Willie more severely than ever). Take that, sir!
Willie (crying more bitterly than ever). Oh, please, sir! — My bottom's so sore!
Please don't, sir — don't whip me, sir, please, any more!
O, I'll never not look at my lesson again —
No, never, sir! Please, sir! Next time, sir — oh, then
I won't ask you to spare me if ever I don't
Know my lesson.
Master (still whipping him). Be sure, Master Wilfred, I won't
I won't spare you, sir, then; you may guess, my boy, how
I shall flog you next time! I won't spare you, sir, now.
You feel, and we see how the birch makes you bleed:
And I hope I shall make you remember it, Reed[.]
I must whip you, sir, very severely indeed,
I see, — and I'm sorry to see it, my lad —
To make you remember the flogging you've had
The stripes you got here, sir — and why, sir, you got 'em
To make any impression at all on your — bottom.
(Whipping Willie again and again, very severely indeed.

Edward (aside). Well, to judge by the old cuts we see, and the fresh 'uns,
I should say that the birch had made lots of impressions
On Willie's unfortunate bottom. By Jove!
What a cut! (seeing Willie's bottom lashed till the blood runs.

Master. Now, the next time you're tempted to move
Out of bounds, or do anything equally silly
When you ought to be getting your lessons up, Willie,
I think (whipping Willie) you'll think twice of it. Eh, Master Reed?
Does the birch (whipping Willie again) make you smart — make you cry — make you bleed,
Does it hurt? (whipping Willie again) Don't you want, sir, to pull down your shirt?
Does it hurt? — Does it hurt? — Does it hurt? — Does it hurt?
Does it hurt? (whipping Willie more & more severely at each fresh cut.

Willie (writhing in agony under the lash). Oh! — Oh! — Oh, sir! — Yes! — Yes!

Master (whipping Willie till the blood runs at each cut). So I thought.
Your plump little rump, my boy, looks as it ought
To look when you take down your breeches each morning
To [bathe] in the burn with your schoolfellows — warning
Other youngsters who sit on the lower boys' form,
And whose bottoms, at sight of your bottom, feel warm,
To take heed — if the rascals will ever take heed —
By the sight of the cuts on your bum, Willie Reed;
By the sight of the stripes there that speak, though you're dumb,
By the sight of the marks of the birch on your bum.
And now — as the birch is worn out — and I know
Your backside must be smarting — take that, my boy,

Willie (with a tremendous howl, as he feels the birch come down on his bottom). **Oh!**

Master. And now, sir, get up; & remember this clearly —
The next time you're whipped, you'll be whipped more severely.
(Willie gets up from the whipping-block in tears & begins
to button up his trousers, crying & sobbing & writhing & rubbing his bottom.

The Flogging-Block. Eclogue V. Charlie's Flogging. 1

Prelude to Charlie's Flogging. I.

Scene, Dr. Birkenshaw's study.
Enter Dr. Birkenshaw & Mr. Armstrong.

A. I wished, sir, to speak to you, simply to say
That I hope you will flog Charlie Clavering to-day.
I have flogged him myself two or three times this half;
But his conduct – what boys call his cheek or his chaff —
Demands, though I've given him some smart castigation,
A more public & much more severe flagellation
Than the lower school ever has seen, or than I
Should feel justified, sir, in inflicting.
B. And why?
A. Well, sir, I would rather you took him in hand.
When he comes — as I trust he will soon come — to stand
Before you, in sight of the whole upper school,
To be punished in public, the stubborn young mule
Will feel — if he didn't, his case would be odd —
That it's best to obey at a word or a nod —
And you'll give him a pretty sharp taste of the rod,
I hope, sir.
B. But why don't you lick the young cub — lick
Him yourself into shape?
A. Sir, a flogging in public
Will be more efficacious by far, & will make
All the lower school boys more alive & awake
To the risk that they run — to the goal that they drive at
By misconduct — than twenty sound floggings in private.

B. Is the lower school private? The youngster who's stripped there
In sight of the youngsters who all see him whipped there
Would hardly agree with you — would they? And you
Can flog pretty hard — as I know that you do —
You can flog pretty smartly: why, sometimes the roars
Of the boys you are flogging are heard through the doors
That divide from the upper the lower school. Still,
If you wish me to whip Charlie Clavering, I will.

A. Sir, there isn't a worse though there's many a slower boy.

B. Then I'll whip him. I never did yet whip a lower boy;
You would surely, I thought, lay the lash on him soundly,
If deserved: but I'll whip Master Charles — whip him soundly.
His brother's example, you know, is so bad
That we can't be surprised if the poor little lad
Who has Algernon Clavering for senior & guide,
Though he sees the birch tickle his brother's backside
So often, should follow his elder, & mock
At all warnings & rules — till he comes to the block.
And now, setting Charlie aside for the present,
Let us just look the flogging-lists over: it's pleasant
And useful — amusing & helpful — to search out
The names of the boys whose backsides wear most birch out.
Hand me over the book, if you please, that contains
The account — the accusing account that remains
When the punishment given is a thing of the past.
Let us see who stands first on the list — & who's last.

Prelude to Charlie's Flogging.

2

A. The old name, sir, of Clavering, I think, will be first.
B. So do I. I don't think Algy Clavering the worst
Of the boys we have here to look after — he's brave
And honest & generous; but then such a slave
To each whim of the moment — the wind & the wave
Are steady, compared to that youngster: & yet
There are times, now & then, when I really regret
To remember how often I've flogged him, & think
How often again I must flog him — I'd wink,
If I could, at his faults now & then: but I fear
He's proud of the fact that no other boy here
Gets punished as often as he — which is clearly
The fact — & no other gets flogged so severely.
Let us look at the register; there we shall find
How often each boy has been tickled behind,
And which boy has most frequently broken the law.
(Reads.
'Algy Clavering' — of course — 'Percy Featherstonhaugh' —
I had really forgotten it. Strange, that the pain
And disgrace of a flogging should all be in vain,
When a big fellow takes down his trousers again
For the hundredth time, shamelessly. 'Redgie Loraine' —
Well, before I had looked at the list here, I reckoned
That Reginald's name would be certainly second
On the roll of disgrace; for I've shown him no mercy
This half; but he hasn't quite matched Master Percy,
Though their records of flogging but slightly have differed.
And now, who's the fourth on the list? — Arthur Clifford.

I thought so — the porter who horses him — Gifford,
You know — when I asked him, replied — Master Clifford?
Eh, weel, sir — except Maister Clavering, of course
(for, ye ken, sir, I'm just that young gentleman's horse —
He bestrides me and rides me, with bottom stripped bare,
Each time he's not whipped on the flogging-block there.)
And except Maister Featherstonhaugh — and I'm fain
To remember how lately ye've whipped him again —
And excepting, of course Maister Redgie Loraine —
If ye ask wha's the sufferer I've oftenest had, sir,
On my back to be whipped — eh, and was not I glad, sir,
Of the task! — I'd reply, Maister Clifford's the lad, sir.

A. Frank Fane, Willie Reed, and Ted Collingwood, ought
To be high on the list, I should surely have thought.

B. So they are. Willie Reed is the fifth of the lot,
Frank Fane is the sixth. His backside must be hot
This morning — though, doubtless, it seldom is not —
For I whipped him at bedtime — just going to bed —
Last night, till his plump little rump was as red
As ever you saw the backside of an older boy.

A. But you never, I think, saw a 'cheekier' or bolder boy:
The more he gets whipped, the more daring he grows.

B. Well, next time he's flogged, Mr. Armstrong, — who knows? —
Perhaps we shall see Master Franky give in:
He's an impudent imp — with a delicate skin.

I'll remember to tickle him well, & pick out
A good cutting fresh rod for him: then, I don't doubt,
We shall see the boy writhing & wincing with pain,
We shall hear the boy roaring again & again
For mercy, before we have done with Frank Fane.
A. I hope so, I'm sure, sir. Who's next on your list
Of whipped bottoms?
B. Ned Collingwood: when has he missed
A chance of incurring such punishment? See!
Algy, Percy, & Redgie at top of the tree —
The birch-tree — then Arthur, Frank, Willie, & he.
No — Willie, Frank, Edward — Ay, that's how they come,
Boy by boy, name by name, & whipped bum by whipped bum.
So, these are the seven who wear out more birch
Than the rest of their schoolfellows, eh? Well, in church
I've observed how uneasy they seem on their seats
Each Sunday. We needn't look further: this meets
Most exactly my confident anticipation. —
Well, Charlie shall have a severe flagellation,
As you wish it, I promise you, Armstrong. Good day.
A. Don't spare the young rascal! Don't spare him, sir, pray!
B. I won't: & to frighten the rascal before
I flog him, I'll flog his big brother once more.
I'll have Algernon horsed while his junior is stripping:
And Charlie shall tingle from Algernon's whipping.

Prelude to Charlie's Flogging
(continued)

II

Scene — the school yard. Enter George Charlton & Charles Edward Clavering, [...]

George. Come here, sir. Come this way, my dear little cousin.
Do you know, sir, they're going to give you nine dozen?
Charlie. No, I don't.
George. But they are — it's as good as a feast
To think of! Or five, — yes, five dozen at least.
Don't you know? You'll be whipped, I would lay a good wager,
As severely — for once — as that jackass your major.
You'll be punished in sight of the whole upper school.
You'll be flogged just as Algy gets flogged, you young fool.
Don't you know you're complained of — by Armstrong?
Charlie. Oh, yes!
George. You've been flogged, I know, often: but now — you can't guess
How the birch-twigs will hurt you. Ask Algernon! Why!
You can't think what the torture is like till you try.
The first cut won't allow you to keep your mouth shut.
He'll cut to the bone. He'll draw blood at each cut.
He'll punish your big brother Algernon first.
I don't know which he'll flog — you or Algernon — worst.
You'll have to look on — won't you tingle, by God! —
While Algernon's bottom grows red from the rod:
You'll see the red mark of each twig & each bud,
Till Algernon's bottom is covered with blood.
You'll hear how he roars, & you'll guess how he feels,
When Algernon's bottom is covered with weals,
And you'll think, at each cut on your brother's backside,
How you'll feel when you ride on the horse that he'll ride.
But when your own breeches are down, you young dog, you,
We shall see, & you'll feel, Master Charles, how he'll flog you!

Charlie's Flogging

Prelude to Charlie's Flogging (continued).

III.

Scene — outside the school. Enter Clavering major & Clavering minor.

Algernon. Why, Charlie, you look rather queer — what's the [row]?
Has any one — Charlton — been bullying you? Now,
Speak up — what's the matter?

Charlie. It is such a shame!

Algernon. You've been swished, eh, in lower school, Charlie? The same
Misfortune — in upper school — sometimes, you know,
Has happened to me.

Charlie. Oh, but, Algernon — Oh,
'Tisn't that — I'm sent up to be swished (just like you)
In the upper school. You're to flogged, they say, too.

Algernon. Very likely. By Jove, it's a shame, though! But why
Does the thought of a flogging, my boy, make you cry?
Ain't as if you had never been stripped before
Other junior boy's eyes — or had never been whipped before.

Charlie. Oh, but Algy, they tell us the swishings you get
Are much worse than a junior has ever had yet.

Algernon. I should hope so; if not, it would really be hard
On the youngsters.

Charlie. They say that your bottom's all scarred
— There were two of our fellows who saw you, I know,
Only yesterday, bathing — it frightened them so
To think of a flogging like that, that it made them
Look out.

Algernon (laughing). Did the sight of my bottom persuade them

To look out for their own little bottoms? By Jove,
What a lark! So they sapped, then — they laboured & strove,
Like good little boys in a jolly funk,
To get up their lessons, & shirk what they shrunk
From the thought of — a duel, or even a parley,
With the birch? But I thought you'd more pluck in you, Charlie
I thought you had really more pluck in you.

Charlie (blushing deeply). Oh!
Do you think I'm a coward, then, Algy? You know
I've never been up in the flogging-room, where
You've been punished so often — &, O, when I'm there,
When I'm down on my knees on the flogging-block — O,
It's because I'm afraid I shall never, you know,
Be able to bear it. I know I shall cry
At each cut of the birch!

Algernon (smiling) Well, my boy, so do I
Quite as often as not. I don't see why one shouldn't
Sing out, if it hurts — if one likes; but one wouldn't
Sing out if it didn't. And sometimes, to tell
The truth, when the master was flogging me well,
I've howled at the very first cut, & implored
Him to spare me, & bellowed, & wriggled, & roared,
And cried till the tears ran all over my face —
Couldn't help it — can't help it — where's the disgrace?

Charlie. Oh, but Algernon, Algernon, tell me — shall I
Be whipped as severely as you were?

Algernon. Don't cry.

Prelude to Charlie's Flogging (continued)

Charlie. Oh, but, Algernon, Algernon, tell me — oh, do —
Am I sure to be whipped as severely as you?
Algernon. My poor dear little chap, how on earth can I tell?
I don't think so — of course. But don't cry so!
Charlie (sobbing). Oh, well,
It's easy to talk! Oh, but wouldn't you cry
If you were no bigger or older than I!
Algernon. Well, I must say, — you force me to say it — you do! —
The first time I was swished I was younger than you,
And I didn't — no, Charlie, I didn't begin
Crying, sobbing, & howling like you, till my skin
Had felt the first taste of the birch on it. Don't
Be a coward — come, Charlie!
Charlie (wiping his eyes). No, Algy, I won't.
But does Birkenshaw flog you as hard as my father
When he flogs you at home in the library?
Algernon (shrugging his shoulders). Rather!
I don't know — but I think, of the two, I would rather,
If I must have a flogging, be flogged by my father.
Charlie. Oh, Algy! And sometimes I've seen him, you know,
Lay the birch on your bottom like anything! Oh!
Algernon. That you have, you young rascal — & sometimes, my lad,
I've thought, when you've seen me well swished, you've been glad
To see him lay into me, Charlie. Now, come,
Don't I know, when the governor tickles my bum,

How you like to be present? he says so himself
To my mother — I've heard him — 'that sharp little elf
Master Charlie does like to see Algernon whipped!
From the moment when Algy began to be stripped
To the moment the birch was laid down, I could see
How Charlie was chuckling & giggling with glee.'

Charlie. O, but how many cuts do you think I shall get?

Algernon. How many's the most you've ever had yet?

Charlie. Eighteen, with two birches; the twigs were all green.
O, he won't — O, he can't give me more than eighteen?

Algernon. Well, I wouldn't just swear that he won't.

Charlie. Oh, I say!

Algernon. Why, what would you think of three dozen, then — eh?

Charlie (crying). O, I think it would kill me — I never could stand
Such a flogging.

Algernon. Well, certainly Birkenshaw's hand
Is heavier & harder than Armstrong's: Frank Fane
Was yesterday saying to me & Loraine
How he wished he was back under Armstrong again.
Three floggings from Armstrong — he wasn't in fun
When he said so — were little or nothing to one
From Birkenshaw. Come now, old fellow, don't cry:
What's the use? You must bear it, my boy; so must I.
And sooner or later you know it must come —
It was certain — the birch & the block & your bum
Were made for each other. It's just hic, haec, hoc!

Charlie. Your bottom was made for the birch & the block,
And the block & the birch for your bottom, I know
Very well — we all know it was, Algernon —

Algernon. Oh!

Charlie's Flogging

(Prelude to Charlie's Flogging — continued)

My bottom is made to be whipped, do you say?
And your bottom was not, Master Charlie, then? Eh?
If you'd said so to Charlton or Featherstonhaugh,
You'd have had a good licking, you know, by the law
Of the school — yes, a jolly good licking. My mother
Made me promise I never would lick my younger brother
At school — or I'd lick you for that — not as Percy
Or George would — oh, Charlie, they'd show you no mercy! —
But I'd lick you.

Charlie. Oh! Why?

Algernon. Never mind — never mind:
You'll catch it in school, sir — you'll catch it behind.
I won't hit you in front — never fear; I won't lick you
Behind: you'll be swished, & it's useless to lick you.
You don't know what you're in for — can't guess what's to come
Won't Birkenshaw tickle & tickle your bum!
He'll tickle it first with a dozen — or nine —
Or eighteen good sharp cuts, as he always does mine;
Then he'll take a fresh birch, & lay into you faster
Till the blood runs, my boy. Ah! you'll find the Head Master
Can make the birch-buds fly about!

Charlie. Well, but you,
Master Algy, will catch it — you're in for it too:
And he spites you, they say. Won't you catch it!

Algernon. That's true.
But you see, Master Charles, I don't funk it — like you.

Charlie. Why, you said just a minute ago that you cried
At each cut of the birch, when your naked backside
Was whipped — 'at the very first cut' & 'implored
Him to spare you' — you know you did, Algy — and 'roared
For mercy' — no wonder! but how can you say,
After that, you don't funk it — don't flinch from it — eh?

Algernon. Well, of course, when one's swished, one don't like it: but then,
If a chap has the courage to face it again,
— Though it isn't exactly his face that he shows
To the master — it isn't his face that the blows
Of the birch-twigs inflame till it tingles & glows
At each cut, & the blood, at each lash on it, flows
In a little red stream —

Charlie (wincing). Oh! I say!

Algernon (laughing). No, it's not
The face that turns red at each stroke, & gets hot,
And smarts till a fellow can't bear it, & cries,
And feels the tears stream down his cheeks, & his eyes
Burn hot with fresh tears at each cut: but, you see,
If a fellow's not cowed though he knows he shall be
Pretty certainly swished again soon — he's a fool,
Very likely — the scoff of the whole upper school,
I dare say — but you can't say he funks it, eh? — Though
I don't say he won't cry under punishment.

Charlie. No.
But I wish it was over!

Algernon. By Jove, so do I!
But you'll try not to cry, my boy, — won't you?

Charlie. I'll try.

Algernon. So will I — but perhaps we shall both of us cry.

(Exeunt ambo)

Charlie's Flogging.

Scene, the public flogging-room in the upper-school. Gifford, the school porter, discovered standing by the flogging-block. Six or seven tough, green, sappy rods, with a copious supply of hard fresh young birch-buds on each twig, are lying side by side on a desk hard by.

Gifford. Eh! don't they just catch it — these dainty young chaps!
The youngest, just fresh from their dear mother's laps,
And the eldest! Won't Algernon catch it, perhaps!
Eh, it's pleasant to see their backsides when the rod
Has warmed them — & wealed them all over, by God!
The sound of the strokes — eh, what musical rhymes!
I have horsed Master Algernon hundreds of times
Since the first he came to school two or three years ago,
And how often they'll whip him again I don't know,
But at least I know this — as I've horsed him before,
I shall horse him for whipping a hundred times more.
Yes, I know Master Algernon Clavering: I'll bet
I shall horse him for whipping some hundred times yet,
He thinks he can bear it: he says he don't mind
A flogging: but, eh! When he's seen from behind,
Undressing, or dressing, or bathing! his bum
Is a pattern: & now Master Charlie must come
To the block — to the flogging-block here. We shall see
If Algernon's brother's as hardy as he.
Ay, it's pleasant to see the young gentlemen stripped
And take them — successively up to be whipped!

Enter Dr. Birkenshaw, followed by George Charlton, Leonard Dacre, Algernon Clavering, Percy Featherstonhaugh, Edward Collingwood, Frank Fane, Arthur Clifford, Wilfred Reed, Reginald Loraine, Philip Dilston, Walter Heron, Frederick Norton, Rupert [Errington], & Charlie Clavering.

Master. Charles Clavering, come forward. Hand out, sir. You know
You're complained of — sent up, sir — sent up from below
For punishment here. This has never occurred
Before — and I thought, I must say, on my word,
That if ever your brother had never incurred
Such disgrace, there would never — there never could be
A boy who would do so — not one, if not he.

Algernon (aside to Percy). He forgets I was never in Lower School.

Percy. Oh!
That explains why you never were flogged there, then.

Master. So,
You see, my young friend, that you must not expect
Much indulgence, considering how little effect
All your past castigations appear to have had
On your conduct — if not on your bottom, my lad.
We shall see what impression the birch-twigs have made
On your skin, pretty soon; but I'm sadly afraid
That the passing impression produced on your mind
By the smart you have hitherto felt from behind
Has been too like a lesson not half got by heart:
But you've ne'er smarted yet as you're going to smart.

Charlie's Flogging.

Ay, you well may clap all your ten fingers behind —
They won't screen your posteriors, my boy — as you'll find,
When the birch is applied to a sensitive part, sir.
No, you never have smarted as now you shall smart, sir.
You shall feel for the first time what Algernon feels
When I flog him, & cover his bottom with weals.
But first you shall see — Philip, hand me some switches down —
What Algernon suffers, when horsed, with his breeches down.
(Philip takes two or three rods off the desk & offers them to the Master.
Ah, these are all really good rods — nice & lithe;
They will make the posteriors that smart from them writhe.
Strong, supple stout rods — not too stout; one can tell
They will sting; & I swish them to sting — to sting well.
Take your breeches down, Algernon. This one, I think,
Is the best. Can you look at it, Charles, & not wink?
The first sight of it made Master Algernon shrink.
Made him wince — made him flinch, as you saw & you see,
Now he's taking his trousers down slowly, that he —
Even he, who is pretty well used to it — feels
Apprehension. Eh, Algy? Just look at the weals
On his bottom — you'll see them as soon as he's stripped
And hoisted — & think, would you like to be whipped
As severely? Come, Algernon, don't keep us waiting.
There's one thing all present agree in in hating
To be kept overlong in prolonged expectation
Of the sight & the sense of a boy's flagellation.

Strip, Algernon! Strip, sir, I say! You can't guess, sir,
How I'll punish you! Will you obey me, sir?

Algernon (beginning to unbutton his trousers). Yes, sir.

Master. And I'll give you, my lad, something bitter to sup. —
Take him up, take him up! Do you hear? take him up.
(Algernon is horsed.
Now, Charlton, Clifford, lay hold of his shirt
Pull it up — higher — higher.

George (aside). By Jove, won't it hurt
When the lash is laid on to those prints of old lashes!
Why, the cuts on the right will be absolute gashes
When the rod makes them bleed again. Eh, what a spree!
Algy Clavering's backside is a picture to see,
With the scars on it. Didn't it smart when it got 'em!

Master. Now, Charlie, look well at your big brother's bottom;
At your brother's big bottom, I might say, perhaps,
as you
Would think — it must seem pretty big to such chaps as you,
And your comrades — big, brawny, broad, pouting & plump —
A stalwart, stout, full-cheeked, great naked white rump.
But observe — you will profit, I trust, by the sight of it —
The weals on the left & the cuts on the right of it.

Charlie (aside, & trembling as he gazes on his brother's bottom). By Jove! — Oh, I say!

George (aside to Charlie). Ah, my lad, a'n't it nuts
To see Algernon hoisted? Ah! look at those cuts!
Why, his bottom is perfectly covered with weals!
Can you guess (for you'll precious soon feel) what he feels?
(The Master begins whipping Algernon.
There! There, Master Charlie! Look there, sir! And there!
Do you see how the birch-twigs bend round on the bare
Tender tingling soft flesh at each stroke? Did you ever
See a whipping like this in the Lower School?

Charlie. Never!

Charlie's Flogging. 9

Charlie. See a whipping like this in the Lower School?
Never!

George. Ah, my 'bonnie Prince Charlie', you see it was true,
What I told you! & soon you'll be feeling it too,
When you're horsed, & the birch is laid well into you!
The proof of my words should be pretty convincing.

Charlie. But Algernon bears it, you see, without wincing.

George. Yes — Algernon *does* bear the pain like a man —
Sometimes, though not always. Do *you* think you can?

Charlie. I don't know; but I'll try.

George. But you'll scarcely succeed.
Did you see how that last cut made Algernon bleed?
The sixth or the seventh — which was it? You start?
Do you see how this fresh cut makes Algernon smart?

Charlie (wincing). Oh! How can he bear it?

George. He won't bear much more
Without crying.

Charlie. He *must* be so awfully sore!
(Algernon writhes.

George. There, you see how the smart is beginning to tell.

Charlie (glancing up timidly at the Head Master). How he does lay it on!

George. Ay — when last the rod fell,
It hit hard. But he always whips Algernon well.
Whenever he gives him a flogging, it *is* one.

Master. Bring a fresh rod, boy — Algernon doesn't like this one,
I can see; & the twigs are all broken — already!
Bring a supple well-budded stout birch for him, Freddy,
(Frederick hands him a rod.

Has this birch been well soaked?

Frederick. Yes, it's fresh from the brine, sir.

Master. Good. — Mark me, now, Clavering: you've had your first nine, sir,
And you don't seem to like them. You've had your first dose,
And the second is coming — it's near you — it's close.
I give you a minute or two to expect
The first cut, that the certain & painful effect
Of the sense of the stinging tough twigs as they come
Sheer down on your smarting great red naked bum
May be all the more keen for the respite you've had,
And your punishment last all the longer, my lad.
Your punishment, Algernon, now may appear,
In the eyes of your brother, a little severe:
But when next your backside & the birchen twigs kiss
He shall see & remember what punishment is.

Charlie (aside). Severe! I should think so! Poor Algy! Poor fellow!
I can't think — I can't think how he bears it so well! O,
I wish it was over, by Jove! I can't bear —
To see it!

George. Look out, Master Charlie, now! There!

(The Master begins whipping Algernon again.

How he makes the buds fly when they've made the blood come!
How he makes the blood spin out of Algernon's bum!

Master (whipping Algernon soundly, with a pause after every cut of the birch).
You didn't much relish — you didn't enjoy
The taste of the birch that I gave you, my boy,
Just now, I'm afraid. Well, is this to your wish?
Do you like this one better? (**Swish!**) Eh, my lad? (**Swish!**)

Charlie's Flogging. 10

Algernon (writhing under the lash). Oh! Oh, I can't bear it!
Master (whipping him severely). But bear it you must.
And the sight will impress your young brother, I trust.
This birch, like the first rod, must give you your nine,
Master Algernon. (**Swish**!) Does you bum feel the brine?
You yourself, sir, are something, you know, of a pickle: you
Ought to know how a rod kept in pickle can tickle you.
Does your bum feel the brine, eh? It shan't be my fault
If it doesn't, my boy. Does it smart from the salt?
(Swish!) Eh? do you feel you've done wrong? do you wish
That you hadn't — eh, Algernon? eh, my boy? (**Swish!**)
(Algernon sobs.
Now, mark me, Charles Clavering. You see what your brother
Is suffering: you see he can't bear it — can't smother
His cries & his sobs — though he's used to it, too —
And, as Algernon smarts from the birch, so will you.
Charlie (bursting into tears). Oh, please, sir! Oh please let me off, sir, for once!
(The Master, after a pause, begins whipping Algernon again.
George (aside to Charlie). You young ass! Now you know how you'll smart, you young dunce!
Reginald (aside). By Jove, it's a shame! It's a beastly black shame
To whip fellows like Algy like that!
George (aside). What a game!
(The Master, after another pause, begins whipping Algernon with redoubled severity.
Look, look, Master Charles! See — don't keep your eyes shut —
How he twists his whipped bottom about at each cut;
How the pain makes him bound — makes him wriggle & jump,
While the birch-twigs are brushing & tickling his rump!

Arthur (aside to Frank). How often has Clavering been tickled this half?
Frank. I'm not sure, but I think thirty-five times.
Arthur. Don't chaff.
Frank. I'm not chaffing a bit.
Arthur. But you must be in chaff.
We're not half through the second month yet of the half.
Frank. Well, & Clavering (by Jove, a'n't he catching it hot!)
Gets oftener swished of a morning than not.
Two days out of three, by the plain computation
Of yesterday's smart & today's castigation,
Algy Clavering is sure of a sound flagellation
Such as seldom has made any other chap's skin burn.
Arthur. Ah, you don't know a cousin of mine — Redgie Swinburne.
There isn't a single boy here — no, there's not —
Who gets it so often & gets it so hot.
Frank. By Jove! Master Swinburne must get a good lot!
Arthur. Ask Algernon Clavering, as soon as the Master
Has done whipping him, Fane.
Frank. He whips faster & faster
And hits harder & harder, if possible. How
Any fellow can bear as he's bearing it now
What Algy's posteriors, each time they receive
A fresh cut, must be suffering, I can't conceive.
Though I see it, by Jove, I can hardly believe
That a fellow can stand it (it's deucedly odd!)
Without howling aloud at each stroke of the rod.
One would think it don't hurt — but I know how it feels,
Look, Clifford — just look at these bloody red weals!

	You don't mean — you, who know how the birch makes one's skin burn —
	That this cousin of yours, Redgie — what's his name? Swinburne,
	Gets whipped more severely than this?
Arthur.	Yes, I do, though.
Frank.	How I should like to see it, by Jove! It's not true, though.
	I believe it's a lie — one can't bear so much pain.
Arthur.	Believe it or not, I can tell you, Frank Fane,
	It's the truth — it's as true as that birch makes the skin burn.
Frank.	Then I'm glad that my name isn't Reginald Swinburne.
	What sort of a chap is your cousin? perhaps
	He deserves it.
Arthur.	Oh no — there are many worse chaps.
	He & Algernon Clavering have always been chums,
	And there always are marks of the birch on their bums.
George	(aside to Charlie). Do you see, my lad — eh? do you see what you'll get?
	And he hasn't half done whipping Algernon yet.
	(Algernon cries & sobs.
	It won't much surprise me, in spite of his plaints,
	I can tell you, if Algy gets flogged till he faints.
Master	(laying down the rod, & addressing the porter).
	Let him go: he has had his first dose. Let him down.
	(The porter releases Algernon, who gets down off his back, crying.
Frank.	How he cries! how he writhes! how the pain makes him frown!
Master.	I shall whip you again, Mr. Algernon, mind,
	When I've tickled young Charles with the birch from behind.
	When your bottom has had some ten minutes of ease,
	The familiar old flogging-block waits for your knees.
Algernon	(writhing with pain). Oh! Oh, I can bear it no longer, sir, please!

Master. That's unlucky my lad; for you'll both have to bear it:
And you know, when the rod is required, I don't spare it.
Double flogging clears up a boy's brains when befogged:
And Charles & yourself shall be both double flogged.
First, hoisted, and whipped on the back of the porter
— And, when horsed, as you know, boy, the birch gives no quarter
— Then, smarting & sore, with your bottom still bare,
Flogged again, and flogged well, — on the flogging-block there.

George (aside). Flogged again, — and flogged well, — on the flogging-block! O,
What a lark! Won't my cousins just catch it! O no!
Double flogged, — flogged in public, — both major & minor, —
Both brothers at once! Won't the pain make them whine
or
Cry aloud at each cut on the bottom, by God!

Master. Now, Charlie, make ready, my boy, for the rod.
(Charlie lets down his trousers.
Take him up. (Charlie is horsed.

George (aside). He's been jolly well swished, I can guess,
In Lower School, often & often; but less
Than he'll now be!

Master. This rod is a stinging one — yes —
It will do, I can see, for another sharp bout
Of whipping; the supple tough twigs will hold out
A bit longer, though frayed here & there — frayed & bruised,
And red as the bottom on which they've been used.

Charlie's Flogging.

	Your big brother Algernon, Charlie, has had
	Twelve cuts with this birch, as you've witnessed, my lad:
	The tips of the twigs are still wet with his blood,
	But still there is left — here & there — a birch bud.
	Twelve cuts, though severe ones, are scarcely enough
	To wear out a fresh rod, if sufficiently tough
	For a naughty boy's bottom: & no one could wish
	For a rod more adapted to tickle the fish
	Than this — as you'll find pretty soon, my boy. **Swish!**
	(Flogs Charlie. Charlie roars with pain at the very first cut.
	No crying, sir! **Swish!** I won't have it!
Charlie	(writhing in agony under the birch). Oh! Oh!
	Oh! Oh!
Master	(flogging him again). I won't have it, I tell you, sir — no!
	A brave boy, though smarting, is dumb as a fish
	Under punishment. Silence, young Clavering!
	Swish! Swish!
	Swish! Swish! (Charlie screams & roars with the pain.
Frank	(aside to Reginald). O, how Birkenshaw does make him bellow!
Reginald.	No wonder: he lashes the poor little fellow
	As hard as he lashed his big brother, almost.
	Well, Charlie will always be able to boast
	That he was the first of the Lower School boys
	Ever punished in Upper School. Hark! what a noise!

The sound of the birch, & the boy's ululations
Under this the severest of all flagellations
That ever excited his loud lamentations,
Contend & alternate like echoes in parley.

Algernon (aside, rubbing his bottom with his shirt, & rubbing his eyes with the sleeve of his jacket). I say, though, he's catching it hot, too, is Charlie!

Master. That makes, I think, six cuts with <u>this</u> rod: each bud on it
Has by this time a stain left of each brother's blood on it.
I can see on the birch-twigs the blood of the taller boy
Now mixed & confused with blood of the smaller boy,
See, my lads, how the birch that chastises boys' tricks cuts!
Algy Clavering had twelve cuts, and Charles has had six cuts,
And each cut has drawn blood from the bare-bottomed brother.
This rod's work is done: some one fetch me another.
(Fred Norton brings him a tough, stout, cutting birch.
Yes, Norton — yes, Freddy, my boy, this will do —
This cut will cut Master Charles to the quick. When were you
Flogged last, Fred?

Fred (blushing). Last week, sir, on Friday.

Master (smiling). Indeed!
And how often this half has the birch made you bleed?

Fred. Eighteen times, I think, sir.

Master. Don't hang down your head.
You think so, my lad? you're not sure of it, Fred?
Can you tell me — you've told one the day when you got 'em —
How many smart lashes were laid on your bottom
Last Friday?

Fred (wincing at the recollection) Oh yes — twenty-one, sir.

Master. No more?
And your bottom would seem to be still rather sore.

13

Charlie's Flogging.

You can't well sit down, Fred, in comfort just yet —
Eh, can you?
Fred (writhing at the idea). O no, sir.
Master. You'll hardly forget
In a hurry, I see, what you suffered when last
You were flogged — though the date of the punishment past
Might have been (as it is not) forgotten, the pain
Is remembered — Take care, Master Redgie Loraine:
Let me hear no more whispering from you or Frank Fane.
Now, Charles, you shall feel what the birch is — as Freddy
Has told us. You fancy you've felt it [already];
Six good hard stinging cuts have drawn blood from your bum:
But you don't know at all, my poor boy, what's to come.
You can't think, my good lad, how you'll smart by and by.
And now you shall see, my boy — now we shall try
How you like it. (Flogs Charlie till the blood runs down.
Charlie (crying & writhing). Oh! Oh, sir! Oh, please, sir!
Master. Don't cry.
Charlie. Oh, please, I can't help, sir! Oh! Oh!
(Charlie receives a fresh cut of the birch at each cry for mercy.
Master. My poor lad,
This is nothing at all to what's coming; you've had
Just twelve cuts in all: now get down. — Let him go.
Charlie. Oh! Oh! How it smarts! How it burns! Oh! Oh! Oh!
(Charlie is let down off the porter's back, crying bitterly.

Master. And now, Mr. Algernon, down on your knees:
Go down on the whipping-block, sir, if you please.

George (aside). He don't like it — but won't he just catch it, by God!

(Algernon kneels down on the whipping-block.

Master. Charles Clavering, stop crying, & look at this rod.
Would you like to know it again? You have felt it, I think,
Six or seven times. The sight makes you tremble & shrink,
I perceive: & the twigs are less neat & less fresh
That when they first saluted your tender young flesh.
Would you know them by sight, eh? you haven't forgot 'em?
Well, now you shall see them whip Algernon's bottom.
Now, Algernon, tuck up your shirt — or do you
Tuck it up for him, George. Very good; that will do.
There's a bottom as red as a father could wish
To see it; but hardly quite red enough. **Swish!**

(The Master begins flogging Algernon again.

Algernon (writhing in agony under the birch). Oh!— Oh! — Oh! — Oh! Oh,
please, sir! — Oh! Oh!

George (chuckling with delight as he looks on). O, by God,
How Algy must smart at each stroke of the rod!
How tremendously hard Dr. Birkenshaw hits!
He'll cut Mr. Algernon's bottom to bits.

Master (whipping Algernon). Does it sting, my lad, eh? does it sting?

George (aside). I should think so!
At each cut of the birch, how he winces & shrinks! O,
How his bottom must tingle each time it gets lashed!
How it makes one's heart leap to see Algernon thrashed!
And Algy is now getting thrashed pretty soundly.
How the Doctor does like whipping Algernon soundly!

Charlie's Flogging.

Master (flogging Algernon severely). I suppose you can't tell me how often, my lad,
I have whipped you this half? all the floggings you've had
Are forgotten, eh, Algernon? are they? And yet
I did think I had given you too much to forget.
I wish I could make you remember; I wish
You would spare me the labour of whipping you (Swish!)
But (Swish!) you don't (Swish!) seem to care or to mind
(Swish! Swish!) what you feel (Swish! Swish! Swish!) from behind.
And yet, by the cries that we hear now & then
When the birch makes you tingle, & tingle again,
And the tears that we see on your face, & the blood
That we see on your bottom, each twig & each bud
Would seem to have hurt you — each stroke as it fell
Would seem to have made your whipped bottom smart well.
Flagellation and Algernon (**Swish!**) must appear
Synonymous terms to the younger boys here:
When they hear but the word flagellation, I guess,
That word must remind them of Algernon. [Yes.]
And when Algernon's name is pronounced, the sensation
It evokes must recall a good sound flagellation;
Or rather, considering that youth's daily rations
Of birch, a many good sound flagellations.
Daily rations of birch have been Algernon's fare
For a fortnight at least, on the whipping-block, where
He is kneeling once more, & exposing a bare
Broad brawny big bottom, as red as his hair,
Or redder, if possible — Algy's red head
Is no redder, perhaps, than another boy's, bred
Of a stock whose red hair is proverbial, it's said:
But where shall we find a boy's bottom as red? (Flogs Algernon again.

Master. Where — where will you see a boy's bottom so scarred,
So wealed with the rod? (Flogs Algernon with redoubled severity.

George (aside). Hit him hard! hit him hard!
Hit him hard, sir! & choose the most sensitive parts
You can find, sir, to flog him on! Oh, how he smarts!
How he smarts at each cut! you can tell by his face
Without looking behind at the seat of disgrace.
Flog him well! flog him well! flog him soundly! Thank God
For the sight of it! Give it him! give him the rod!
Lay it into him well! lay it into him soundly!
Flog him well! make him smart! make him smart! flog him soundly!
Look at Charlie now, Frank: don't the spectacle scare him!
Flog Algernon well, sir! Flog, flog, & don't spare him!

(The Master leaves off flogging Algernon for a few minutes, during which not a sound is heard but Algernon's bitter sobs, as he writhes on the flogging-block in a perfect agony of smart. The burning tears continue to stream down his cheeks in spite of his utmost efforts to suppress them. Gradually, however, he contrives to succeed in hushing up his sobs — dries his tears on the sleeve of his jacket — and, leaning well forward over the whipping-block, prepares himself for a fresh instalment of flagellation, & presents his well whipped & well wealed bottom to the coming cuts of a fresh birch rod without flinching.)

Philip (aside to Reginald). I say, can you tell me, Redgie, my lad,
By the look of him, how many cuts he has had?

Reginald. I've counted them all on my fingers. What fun!
When Algy was horsed, he had just twenty-one;

Nine cuts, well laid on, to begin with; & then
Twelve jolly good cuts on the bottom again
With a jolly good birch-rod made supple with brine:
And this time he's had — let me see, Philip — nine;
Nine good sound hard cuts on his bottom — as hard
As the Doctor can strike; & you see how it's scarred —
You see how each twig in the rod, and each bud
On each twig in it, — look at his bum! — has drawn blood;
How each cut on his bottom has made the blood come.
Well, I wouldn't be Algernon! Look at his bum!
(The flogging begins again.
The Doctor, severe as he always has been to him! —
By Jove, I say, Phil, how he is laying into him! —
Doesn't often — he loves flogging Algernon dearly,
But he doesn't — flog Algernon quite so severely
As he's flogging him now: the boy's fainting, or nearly,
Poor fellow, as sure as my name is Loraine.
Look, Philip, his eyes are quite dim with the pain.
Master (pausing — to take breath — in the process of flagellation, after giving
Algernon three very severe cuts). Do you see, Master Charles, how each twig & each bud
Has flecked Master Algernon's bottom with blood[?]
How he's grinding his teeth like a dog when it snarls
To avoid crying out with the pain of it, Charles?
Look first at his bottom; then look at his face:
And remember you'll soon be in Algernon's place;
In a very few minutes, my boy, by the clock,
You'll find yourself down on your knees on the block
— A sight which the lads looking on will enjoy —
With your breeches down, Charles, & your shirt up, my boy.

The whipping-block here on which Algernon kneels
And exposes a bottom all crimsoned with weals
Is familiar to all the boys present but you:
And you shall be presently whipped on it too.
On the very same block on which Algernon smarts
You shall suffer, & bleed in the very same parts
That he bleeds in so often for daily misdeeds:
You shall bleed on the block on which Algernon bleeds.
You never as yet, Master Charlie, have felt
What he feels: where he's kneeling you never have knelt.
He has knelt there some hundreds of times, & been whipped
Each time pretty smartly: the parts you see stripped
Have often been seen by each other boy here,
And as red as they now are from stripes as severe
As these — and will often again be, I fear.
But you will take warning, I hope: and I wish
I could hope that your idle big brother would. **Swish!**
Don't you think, Master Charlie, your brother must wish
That he wasn't once more on the whipping-block? **Swish!**
Would you like, do you think, Master Charles — would you wish
To be whipped as severely as Algernon? **Swish!**
If he doesn't cry out, do you think he don't wish
That the birch was not here hanging over him? **Swish!**
And he knows, if he only would act as I wish,
That he never would smart on the whipping-block. **Swish!**
He knows in his heart that I heartily wish
I had not to flog him so frequently. **Swish!**
But if Algernon will not behave as I wish
Why, Algernon's bottom must smart for it. **Swish!**

Yes, Algernon's bottom must smart for it. **Swish!**
Yes, Algernon's bottom must smart: though I wish
He himself would take pity upon it — I wish
He would keep himself clear of the whipping-block. **Swish!**

George (aside). Yes, Algernon's bottom must smart! O, by God,
How it must, at each cut of this buddy fresh rod!
How the twigs bend & break on his brawny bare bum!
How each bud makes the blood at each touch of it come!

Algernon (writhing with pain but trying to keep down his sobs). Oh! Oh, sir! Oh, please!

Master (flogging him soundly). Yes, I please, sir, to give you
Your deserts. You'll remember as long as you live, you
Young rebel; I hope & I think so, at least
This flogging: enough is as good as a feast,
They say, & I mean, sir, to give you enough.
These twigs, though the buds are all sappy & tough
And the sprays & the tips of them prickly & rough,
Are beginning to break & wear out, & a fresh
Stout birch will be good for your tender young flesh.
George bring me some rods. — This is pliant & supple.
But this has more buds on it: here is a couple
Of ticklers [—] ay, these will hurt more than the others:
Ay, this will do nicely for both of the brothers.
Master Algernon Clavering's posteriors have had
A taste of three birches — eh, Algy, my lad? —
Two fresh from the brine, & the third of them fresh
From exercise (**Swish!**) on his brother's bare flesh.

But this one, the fourth one, that Algernon feels
Now, (**Swish!**) ought to raise quite a crop of fresh weals —
Quite a harvest of tingling thick throbbing long fresh
Great bloody red smarting sore weals on his flesh.
How it shrinks from the twigs of the birch as they strike it!
Do you like it, sir? (**Swish!**) do you like — do you like it?
(**Swish! Swish!**) Ah, they call you, sir, Algy the Fish,
Because of your passion for swimming: but (**Swish!**)
I won't, sir, I won't have you dumb as a fish
Under punishment here on the flogging-block. (**Swish!**)

Algernon (sobbing). Oh! Please, sir! Oh! Oh, sir!

Master (flogging him soundly). So, Algy the Fish
Can cry out when the rod has just tickled him? (**Swish!**)
Does it sting, sir? I wish, Master Algy, I wish
You would spare me the trouble of whipping you (**Swish!**)
So often each week of the half — for it's daily
My duty to whip you each time more severely —
To whip you, sir, all the more soundly, when stripped,
Because of the number of times you've been whipped.
Now you hear, my boys, all of you, Algy the Fish
Singing out as the rod strikes the tail of him. (**Swish!**)
As the rod strikes the tail — the great wriggling red
tail of him, —
You hear the loud sobbing long pitiful wail of him.
(**Swish! Swish!**) Ah, this rod is just made for this fish!
Eh, Algernon? isn't it, Algernon? (**Swish!**)

Algernon (writing under the torture of the birch). Oh! — Oh!
Master. Do you see, boys, how Algy the Fish
Jumps, — wriggles, — twists, — writhes, — at the touch of it?
Swish! (Applying the blood-stained birch
(once more, with all his force,
Algernon (writhing in agony). Oh! Oh! (to Algernon's bare & bleeding bottom.
Master. Now get up, & stop crying my lad;
And try to remember the whipping you've had.
(Algernon gets up from the whipping-block
With the tears streaming down his cheeks;
Rubs his bottom well with his shirt; draws up
His breeches, & begins to button them up, still
Sobbing bitterly, & writhing with pain.
George (aside). Well, this is a sight that I wouldn't have missed! I'm
Glad to see how the birch has warmed Algernon this time[,]
Has warmed his bum thoroughly well, & performed
Its office. Yes, Algy's bum has been well warmed!
Did you notice, I say, Master Charles, — did you see
How at each cut that made the blood spin from it he
Writhed, quivering & shuffling from shoulder to knee
As he knelt on the flogging-block? Ay, & the Master
Didn't flog him too fast, Charles; he might have flogged faster,
But then Master Algernon wouldn't have felt
The full sting of each cut — the full smart of it, dealt
With the Doctor's whole strength on his bum as he knelt
Where you must kneel now for the first time, & feel
How the birch-twigs warm your backside as you kneel.

You'll feel what your brother has felt: &, by God,
You won't like it all — you won't relish the rod
When it tickles your tender young bottom afresh
And plants some more buds in the smarting soft flesh.
Do you see how you're making old Birkenshaw fawn
By delaying to kneel, eh?

Master (holding up the rod). Charles Clavering, go down.

Charlie (in tears). Oh, please, sir! Oh, do let me off, sir — do, please!
I'm so sore, sir!

Master. Go down, my boy — down on your knees.
It's the first time, I know, that you've done so up here:
But it won't be the last time by many, I fear.
Go down. (Charlie lets down his breeches again, & kneels.

George. Shall I hold up his shirt, sir?

Master Of course.
It's the first time that Charlie has ridden the horse
Which has carried his brother so often, & will
I've no doubt, carry Algy much oftener still.
The horse which the horseman who mounts it must ride
Without breeches or shirt on to screen his backside;
And none could be fitter to act as his groom
Than his cousin. — Stand back there, Frank Fane, & make room
For the sweep of the birch — for the sweep & the swing of it —
That the youngster's posteriors may feel the full sting of it.
(Flogs Charlie soundly.

Charlie. Oh! Oh, sir! Oh! Oh! I can't bear it! Oh! Oh!

Algernon (standing forward). If you please, sir

Master. What now,
Master Algernon? No.

Algernon — Whatever it is, I won't hear you: I've had
For this morning enough of you, Algy, my lad

Algernon (persisting). Please, sir, may I take it for Charlie — the
rest of it —
The rest of his flogging?

George (aside). Come, this is the best of it —
The best of it all! What was ever like this?
By Jove, what an ass Master Algernon is!

Algernon. If you please, sir, I'll take it instead of him. Please,
Do let me, sir! (beginning to unbutton his breeches again.

Arthur (aside). Algy, you fool!

Master. On your knees,
Master Algernon, instantly! Charlie, my lad,
Get up — for the present: get up [...]
[...] cuts [...] shall [...]
[...] cuts are to come & [...]
At each cut I don't doubt — at each cut [...]
[...] will be but the [...]
[...] of [...]
[...] that [...]
[...] from the rod [that] has wealed his [bare] flesh
[...] afresh.
That's all that you'll get — no [...] for [transgression,]
[...] brother's well-meant intercession.
(Charlie gets up off the [whipping-block.]
[Stand there], with your trousers down, Charles, in disgrace:
And, Algernon, come & kneel down in his place.
(Algernon kneels down on the flogging-block
[and lifts] his shirt.

You've had sixty smart strokes of the birch, and you wish
For some more good hard cuts, do you, Algernon? **Swish!**
Swish! Swish! (laying on the birch with all his might.

Algernon (sobbing bitterly at each stroke). Oh! Oh! Oh! 63

Master (whipping him severely). Look at Algy the Fish! 64
Swish! Look at him! Swish! Swish! Swish! 68
Look at him! Swish! 69
Don't you care, Master Algernon? — Swish! Don't you care? [70]
Swish! Swish! [...]

Reginald (aside to Arthur). Oh, I say! O, by Jove, it's not fair!

Arthur. Well, I do think it's rather hard lines — & I wish
It was over.

Master. Take that, sir! And that, my boy! Swish!
Swish! Swish! And take that, Mr. Algernon! Come,
Do you like it, sir?

Algernon (suppressing his sobs). No, sir.

Master (with a very severe cut). It hurts you? Your bum, [...]
Which has worn out so many birch rods, my boy, feels
Pain still when the twigs raise a crop of fresh weals?
You have still, sir, some feeling — although you've been stripped
So often, & scourged — in the parts that are whipped?
Eh, Algernon? eh, my lad? Swish! Don't you wish [80]
Your bum was quite hard, sir — insensible? Swish!
Swish! Swish! So, 'you'll take it instead of your brother,' boy?
All the worse for your own bare backside: & the other boy
Won't smart a bit less for your chivalrous wish
To suffer instead of him, Algernon. Swish!

(Applying the birch to Algernon's bottom so hard as to break the twigs.
[...] 84 cuts

Charlie's Flogging.

And now, Master Algernon — now that you've had
Seven dozen laid on pretty smartly, my lad,
And your bottom is covered with blood & with weals,
Are you sorry or not?

Algernon (taking breath & looking up). Not a bit, sir.

Master (smiling). It feels
Quite pleasant — all right, I suppose, my boy?

Algernon (pulling down his shirt, & rubbing his bottom). No, sir.

Master. And yet you're not sorry for braving me so, sir?

Algernon. No, please, sir — I can't say I'm sorry for trying
To take it (I'm sorry I couldn't help crying)
Instead of my minor, if that's what you mean.

Master. I shall have to invest in a flogging-machine
For your special behoof, Master Clavering, I see,
Or you'll weary my arm out. Get up, sir — & be
More careful henceforward — more mindful of me.
(Algernon gets up again off the whipping-block.
Now, Charles, though you've often seen Algernon stripped before,
Have you ever, my boy, seen him quite so well whipped before?

Charlie (trembling). No, never — not quite, sir.

Master (smiling). And how would you like
To be just as well whipped as that stubborn young tyke
Your perverse elder brother — eh, Charlie, my lad? —
To have just such a scourging as Algy has [had?]

Charlie (with tears in his eyes). Oh, please, it would almost half kill me — it would!
O, I will be a good boy — I'll try to be good!

Master. No, no, Master Charlie: the birch won't half kill you:
It will hurt you, no doubt: it will flog you until you
Are a good boy. You'll try to be good, my lad, will you?

Well, you know, Master Charlie, you've only to try,
And you can. Take your breeches down, now, & don't cry.

Charlie (with tears streaming down his cheeks). O, please, sir, don't
whip me, sir, please, any more!
O, please, sir, my bottom's so awfully sore!

Master. Go down, Master Charlie, this instant. Go down.
Don't stand making faces all day like a clown. (Charlie kneels.
Lift your shirt. (Charlie obeys. The Master flogs him soundly.

Arthur (to Reginald, aside.) Serve him right for a mischievous cub: he
Deserves a good switching. And isn't he chubby!
What a plump little bottom! what stout little thighs!
What a bum for the birch! And by Jove! how he cries!

(The Master gives Charlie six severe cuts of the birch.

Charlie. Oh! Oh! Oh! (Charlie pulls his shirt down & rubs his bottom.

Master. Lift your shirt again, Charles — lift your shirt.

Charlie (sobbing). Oh, it hurts me so! Oh, sir! O! O! how you hurt!

Master. Lift your shirt. (Charlie again obeys, & is again soundly flogged.

Reginald (to Arthur, aside). What a shame! Such a youngster! the pain's
Too sharp for a small boy — a taste of the cane's
Sharp sting on his hand is enough. Why, Frank Fane's
Bare backside isn't redder — not even Frank Fane's —
Than poor Charlie's.

Arthur. And how about Redgie Loraine's?

Reginald. O, my bottom's all right now — the cuts are all healed,
Or nearly. By Jove, though, just wasn't it wealed!

Arthur. Look, Redgie, it's over — he lays down the rod.
But haven't both brothers just caught it, by God!

(Charlie gets up from the whipping-block crying & sobbing.

Master. Stand there, Master Charles — Master Algy, stand there,
You have each had a pretty sharp dose, boys — a fair
Division of suffering — each brother his share.
You will hardly forget it as long as you live,
I should hope lads. Remember, I never forgive.
There's plenty of birch here, mind, always in stock:
And I hardly need bid you remember the block. (Exeunt omnes.

The Flogging-Block. Eclogue VI. Edward's Flogging.

Scene — the private flogging-room.
Enter the Master (Dr. Birkenshaw) and Edward Collingwood.

Master. Do you know why I've sent for you, eh? Can you guess, sir,
Why I sent Algy Clavering to summon you?
Edward. Yes, sir.
Master. You do: Very well, Then, no doubt, you guess
What you to expect, Edward Collingwood.
Edward. Yes.
Master. Well, what, sir?
Edward (sullenly). A flogging.
Master (smiling). This half — as I guess
I have flogged you already some twenty times.
Edward (still more sullenly). [...]
Master. More than twenty times, Collingwood — [...]
Edward (more sullenly than ever). I don't know sir: [...]
Master. Well, Edward, my lad
You've forgotten how many good floggings you've had
You say: it seems so. Go down, sir, & strip! you
[shall] find, Master Edward, [...]
(Edward unbuttons his trousers [...]
Go down on the flogging-block now, sir — kneel down; [...]
And turn up your shirt. (Edward takes his shirt up.
You were larking up town
Last week, I remember — the marks are still red
That remind me — & weren't you well-whipped for it, Ned?

Edward's Flogging

Edward (in a more hopeful voice). Oh, yes, sir — you swished me, sir, awfully.
Master (smiling again). — Wishing
To improve you.
Edward (in a rather whining voice). You gave me, sir — O, such a swishing!
Master. But that flogging, & all other floggings you've had,
Are nothing compared to the flogging, my lad,
Which I'm going to give you. Your schoolfellows, dogging
Your steps, will remind you — if memory needs jogging —
That they will never forget Edward Collingwood's flogging.
Long after the smart & the torture is part of it,
You will writhe — for you will never, my lad, hear the last of it.
You shall pay for your idleness dearly, sir — dearly;
For I'll flog you [severely], sir — very severely.
Edward (springing up off the whipping-block, and
falling on his knees before the Master in an agony of terror).
Oh, don't sir! I'll never be idle! I won't, sir!
But do let me off, sir! Don't flog me, sir! don't sir!
Don't whip me like Percy and Algernon, please sir.
Don't whip me! — Don't whip me. (crying & sobbing with fright.
Master. Get up off your knees, sir!
Stand up, & kneel down again — there, where already
You have knelt down so often for punishment, Teddy.
And now must kneel down for a flogging once more —
On the flogging-block, Collingwood — not on the floor.
Edward (springing up, & kneeling down again, on the whipping-block).
O, yes, sir! I will, sir! But please, sir — I won't
Be late again, ever! Don't flog me, sir! Don't!

Master (taking up one rod after another, and examining them carefully,
rod by rod). Not only, my boy, will I flog you — be sure of it —
But I'll give you as much as your skin can endure of it.

Edward (springing up again off the whipping-block, and falling
on his knees before the Master in a fresh agony of terror).
Oh, do let me off, sir — do, please! I can't bear
What Algy & Percy can, please, sir!

Master (selecting a tough & cutting birch). Well, there
Is an excellent reason, my lad, why you should
Be taught how to bear it — or how to be good.
Go down once again on the whipping-block, Teddy —
Don't keep the birch waiting — we've waited already.
(Edward, still crying bitterly, resumes his position on the whipping-block.
Keep your shirt up, my boy — I suppose you don't wish
For a cut or two extra — eh, Collingwood? **Swish!**
(Applying the birch to Edward's naked bottom with great severity.

Edward (with a sharp cry of agony). Oh! Oh, sir! Oh! please, sir!

Master (again applying the birch to Edward's bottom). It hurts, eh? I'm glad
To see — as I do — (whipping Edward again) how it hurts you, my lad.

Edward. Oh! Oh!

Master (whipping Edward's bottom with increased severity at each cut
of the birch). Yes, I thought you would hardly enjoy
Such a taste of the birch as you're getting, my boy.
And, mind, though your bottom smarts now, what you've had
Is nothing compared to what's coming, my lad.
I'll make you remember the flogging-block.

Edward (writhing & sobbing). Oh, sir!
I will — but, oh, do let me off, sir — do!

Master (flogging Edward very severely). No, sir. (Edward howls with pain.

Edward's Flogging

Take that, Sir! — Take that, Sir! — Take that, Sir!
(Flogging Edward so severely as to draw blood at each cut.

Edward (writhing in agony under the torture). Oh! Oh!
I can't bear it!

Master (flogging his bottom soundly). And yet — you must bear it, you know.
Your skin is no tenderer than other boy's skins
Who have smarted again and again for their sins:
Your flesh is no softer than other boys' flesh
Who again and again have been punished afresh,
And have borne it — in time —without wincing. I wish
I could see you behaving as gallantly. **Swish!**
(Flogging Edward's bottom with all his strength at every cut.
If you move — if you stir — if you pull your shirt
To rub your bare bottom across with the skirt,
You shall feel — & remember — how birch-twigs can hurt,
Master Edward. (Flogging him very severely indeed.

Edward (wincing under the birch at each cut). Oh! Please, sir! Oh! Oh!

Master (whipping his bottom soundly). Stop that noise!
Stop that noise, sir, I tell you! I will not have boys
Cry & howl under punishment, Edward — I won't!
(Whipping Edward's bottom till the blood runs at every cut.

Edward (writhing with pain). Oh, please, sir, don't, please, sir! Don't! Spare me, sir! Don't!

Master (whipping him afresh). 'Don't spare me, sir — don't,' do you say? You enjoy
Being whipped? No, indeed, I won't spare you, my boy!

Edward's Flogging

Edward (writhing with pain at every cut of the birch). Oh! Oh, sir!
Master (whipping him severely). You don't seem to like it, my lad!
But, Collingwood, mark me — the stripes you have had
Are not all, sir: the cuts that you smart from already
Are about half of the dose that's in store for you, Teddy.
But, however, I'll give you a minute or two
To take breath in — a respite before we renew
The duel between your backside & the birch.
Misbehaviour in school & misconduct in church
Have deservedly brought you to trouble, my lad,
Many times before this time: & now you have had
Just a taste of the birch —
Edward (aside). Just a taste of it! Oh!
And my bottom's all bloody by this time, I know!
Master. Just a taste — you don't quite seem to relish it. Eh, Ned?
Edward (in tears). Oh, let me get up from the whipping-block!
Master (selecting a fresh, green-budded stout & supple rod). Nay, Ned —
You can scarcely expect me to let you get up
Till you've drunk to the bottom the dregs of the cup
Of well-merited punishment. Nay — 'twould be odd
If I did so. Now, Edward, just look at this rod.
(Edward looks up, still crying bitterly; the Master shows him the rod.
I don't think I need use on you more than a couple
Of birches to-day. Is it springy, and supple,
And sappy, and buddy, and pliant, and lithe?
Don't you think it will hurt you, my boy — make you writhe?
Edward (sobbing bitterly, and wincing at the sight of the birch).
Oh yes, sir — unless you'll forgive me the rest
Of my punishment. Do, sir! Do, please, sir! I guessed,

Edward's Flogging

When you told me to stay after school-time, you know,
That you'd give me no end of a flogging — but, O,
I didn't — Oh, please, sir! — I couldn't, sir, guess
That you'd flog me like this! I can't bear it, sir!
Master (giving Edward's naked bottom a very severe cut of the birch). Yes,
I thought, Master Edward, the birch, when applied
Like this (whipping him) — & like this (whipping him again) — to your brawny backside,
Would startle you. Well, do you know what the sight
Of your pain makes me feel? (whipping him again.) — That I haven't done right
In sparing you hitherto.
Edward (aside). Sparing me! Oh!
Master (flogging him again). I have punished you often & often, I know;
Master Edward — your bottom bears witness how often
And how soundly; you need not suppose you can soften
My heart by the sight of the weals on your bum,
The sore places, red ridges, & cuts on it: Come,
Don't you think — though they think you at home & at school
A clever boy, Ned — don't you think you're a fool
To provoke me to punish you — eh, my boy? eh? (Whipping him.
Speak up, Master Edward; what have you to say? (Whipping him again.
Not a word? (whipping him again.) Not a word? (whipping him again) Not a word? [Stop] fears
(whipping him again.
That you're hardly as ready with words as with tears. (Whipping him again.
With tears, when well whipped, we all know that you're ready:
But scarcely with words — except foolish ones, Teddy. (Whipping him again.
Speak up —are the birch-twigs you're smarting from tough? (Whipping him again.
Are the knots on them hard? (whipping him again) — are the buds on them rough? (Whipping him again.
Do you think, on the whole, you've had whipping enough? (Whipping him very severely indeed.
Edward (writhing under the birch). Oh! Oh, sir! Oh, please, sir! O yes, sir — I do, sir!
Master. But I cannot agree — on that subject — with you, sir. (Whipping Edward more severely than [ever]. [36]

Edward's Flogging 3

Edward (roaring under the rod). Oh, let me get up, sir!
Master (whipping his bottom). No, Collingwood — no:
Not just yet, my good fellow.
Edward. Oh, please, sir!
The birch (as it comes down again on Edward's bottom). **Swish!**
Edward (crying & screaming). Oh!
Master. Well, you've had your first dose: there's a second dose ready:
But first let me have a few words with you, Teddy.
If you really can't bear being birched, as it seems
By your crying, your writhing, your sobs, & your screams.
It seems to me, Edward, remarkably odd
That you take no more care to keep clear of the rod.
Day after day, as you very well know,
You provoke me to punish you, Edward.
Edward (trying to suppress his sobs). Oh! Oh!
Master. If you cry when you've nothing to cry for, my boy,
When I give you a respite from pain to enjoy
For a minute, — a respite that others might sigh for —
You shall soon, Master Edward, have something to cry for.
Your bottom is tender — the birch-twigs are tough —
But I see you have never been punished enough.

Edward's Flogging

(Whipping Edward again.) Take that as a taste of the whipping to come.
(Edward writhes.
Your head was the sinner — the sufferer's your bum.
Your idle, irresolute, reckless young head
Has led you astray as you should not be led;
And a sharp retribution is this that has come
On your brawny big blushing broad bloody bare bum.
Don't you think so? Your bottom is usually red —
There are plenty of ridges & stripes on it, Ned,
Almost always — I seldom have seen you, when stripped,
Without signs here & there that you'd lately been whipped;
Whipped soundly — whipped smartly — whipped sharply —
Whipped well: (He whips Edward again.
Whipped! Whipped, sir, like this!
(He whips Edward again & again, very severely indeed.
Edward (screaming & roaring with the pain). Oh! — Oh! Oh!
Master (laying the lash on Edward's bottom with all his strength [...]
How it hurts you — can see how it stings you, my lad:
I can see when I cut to the quick: & I'm glad
To know that you feel that you've got your deserts, sir!
(He whips Edward's bottom till the blood runs down.
Edward (writhing). Oh, it hurts me so! Oh! You don't know how it hurts, sir!
Master. Yes, Edward, I do, my boy; I can tell

Edward's Flogging

(Whipping Edward's bottom) How it hurts — I myself have
been often whipped well:
At your age I was constantly whipped: I have bled
On the whipping-block oftener that you, Master Ned:
I've been whipped on the very same whipping-block where
You have now had four dozen — or thereabouts. There
Dr. Roddam, my late predecessor in rule,
Has whipped me so often before the whole school
That I know pretty well how it hurts, & can tell
That you'll live, sir, to thank me for whipping you well.
Yes, my boy; you'll be thankful, in ten years to come,
To the rod that so often has tickled your bum
When you knelt on the block in a beaten boy's attitude;
You'll remember your numberless floggings with gratitude.
The grown man will most surely remember the beaten boy, —
The boy so much oftener whipped than an Eton boy.
I remember full well the last flogging I had:
This flogging's a joke to that flogging, my lad.
Nine dozen I got — yes, a dozen times nine.
Don't you think, now, your flogging's a trifle to mine?
You've had floggings enough — but you've clearly forgot 'em:
Six rods, one by one, were worn out on my bottom
The last time my schoolmaster flogged me: I wish
He were here, sir, to help me in flogging you!

Edward's Flogging

The birch (as it comes down again on Edward's naked bottom). **Swish!**
Edward (roaring with the pain). Oh, but, please, sir! You say, sir, you know how it hurts;
Oh, then, please, sir, please, spare me!
Master (whipping his bottom). You'll get your deserts,
Master Edward, before you get up.
Edward (with tears streaming down his cheeks). I can't bear it!
Oh! Oh!
Master (whipping him again). You can't bear the birch rod? I can't spare it.
I can't spare you one twig of it, Collingwood. There! (whipping him.
I can't spare you one stroke of it; why should I spare
A boy who deserves to be summoned and stripped
Each day of the half, & who ought to be whipped
And who would have been whipped more severely by far —
More severely, take notice, my boy, than you are
Being whipped — more severely by far, you young fool! —
In the days when your father & I went to school —
When we used to be sent for each morning, and stripped,
And whipped on the flogging-block — whipped, my lad, — whipped!
Whipped, Edward — whipped, whipped, Master Collingwood! Then
— Your father Sir Charles must remember it — when
He & I were complained of, as truant or dunce,
We were whipped, Master Edward — whipped soundly; & once,
When Charles Collingwood, smarting, just muttered out — 'God damn!'
He was whipped so severely by good Dr. Roddam
For swearing, while still under punishment — Ah!
You know how I whipped Percy Featherstonhaugh
Last week — you were whipped, I remember, my lad,
On the evening before: don't you think, sir, he had
A good flogging? You rather would wish, I should guess, sir,
To avoid such a flogging as Percy's?
Edward (crying with pain & fear). Oh, yes, sir!

Edward's Flogging

Master (flogging Edward again till the blood runs down).
Well, Edward, that flogging was little or rather
Was nothing compared to the flogging your father
Received: all his schoolfellows witnessed the scene:
I remember his age was exactly sixteen:
A great hulking young fellow he was, too — the cock
of the school — but incessantly punished: the block
Was worn perfectly smooth by Charles Collingwood's knees
As we all used to say: & his bum by degrees
Grew so callous to birch & so hardened with whipping
That he sometimes would grin at his comrades while stripping
For punishment: still, I'm mistaken, my lad,
If he does not remember the flogging he had
That morning. He couldn't sit down for three days.
His bottom was perfectly flayed — as one flays
A carcase: the sight of his broad nether cheeks
Was a warning: he couldn't sit down for three weeks
In comfort; he told me so. Nay, as he sat,
You could see how it hurt him. What think you of that?

Edward (in the tone of a boy who plucks up courage, not having received a lash for the last two or three minutes, though still smarting so severely from the recent application of the rod that he speaks in a hoarse broken voice). I think it was awfully cruel: I do, sir!

Edward's Flogging

Master (flogging Edward so severely as to draw a little stream of blood at each cut).
And perhaps you consider me cruel to you, sir?
Edward (boldly, though flinching with pain). Yes, I do, when you flog me like this.
Master (flogging him again and again and again). Oh, indeed!
When the strokes of the birch make you tingle & bleed,
When your bottom gets rather the worst of the duel
Between bottom and birch, you consider it cruel?
But I'll tell you who wouldn't, my boy — who would rather
Rejoice, for your sake, in your flogging, — your father.
He told, the day that he first brought you here,
How well he remembered the pain & the fear
That all boys must endure in their school education —
The pain & the fear of severe flagellation.
(Edward writhes.
He begged me to flog you whenever I thought
You deserved it, & flog you as hard as you ought
To be flogged — you remember his words, I dare say —
To flog you as soundly as he, when at school,
Had been flogged. 'Ned is just such another young fool
As I was, & wants as much flogging,' he said:
So I know I shall please him by flogging you, Ned.
You see there's no chance of escape for your bottom (Edward sobs.
While those words — neither you, sir, nor I have forgot 'em —
Are remembered. Your father's most sensible wish
Shall be gratified, Edward. Take that, my boy! (**Swish!
Swish! Swish!**) Your plump haunches were getting to fat —
Take that, sir! And that, sir! And that, sir! And that!
(Swish! Swish!) And take that! (flogging Edward soundly.
Edward (writhing under the lash). Oh! Oh, please, sir! — Oh! — Oh!
Master (giving Edward the hardest cut of all at parting).
Now, Edward, get up; put your clothes on; and go.[63]

The Flogging-Block. Eclogue VII Frank's Flogging.

Scene, the public flogging-room. Present — the Head Master
(rod in hand), Algernon, Wilfred, Edward, Philip, Reginald,
Arthur, ^ Hugh, Percival, George, ^ Edwin, Leonard, Frederick, & Frank.

Master. Frank Fane, take your trousers down.
Frank (in an imploring voice of appeal). Please, sir, what for?
Master. For a flogging. Now don't keep me waiting, sir — or —
(Holding up the rod significantly.
Frank. Oh, please, sir — I'm sure I don't know what I've done, sir,
To be whipped again, please, sir, so soon, sir.
Master. Not one, sir,
But many offences — your sleeping in church,
Among other things — call for a taste of the birch.
I'll whip you: I'll make you remember the pain.
Take your trousers down — take down your trousers, Frank Fane.
Frank. Oh, spare me, sir! please, sir, do spare me this once!
Master. I won't spare you: I never did yet spare a dunce.
Frank. Oh, my bottom's so tender, sir, still! It's so sore!
Master. A good reason for whipping your bottom once more.
If the last flagellation I gave your posteriors
Has not taught you, my lad, to respect your superiors
And behave yourself better thereafter, pursuant
To orders — I never did yet spare a truant,
Frank Fane; & I certainly shall not begin
With you, Master Francis. The scrape you are in
Must be chronicled, Frank, on your delicate skin.

— Must be registered, Fane, in red ink, on a leaf
Supplied by yourself with reluctance & grief.
I won't spare you: I never did yet spare a thief,
Stealing apples, you think, is no theft, it would seem.
I'll flog you, Frank Fane, till I've made the blood stream!
I shall punish a truant, a thief, and a dunce,
By flogging Frank Fane, all in one, and at once.
And though Frank, when I flog him, will feel some smart pain,
I shall feel still more pleasure in flogging Frank Fane.
I shall punish a truant, a dunce, & a thief,
By flogging Frank Fane till his bum's like raw beef:
I shall do but my duty — it may be, in vain —
But I'll do it — I'll do it — in flogging Frank Fane.
I shall give all the others a lesson to study
By flogging Frank Fane till his bottom's all bloody:
I shall give the whole school a good lesson what pain
Naughty boys have to look for, by flogging Frank Fane.
Strip, Frank. Now, my boys, you shall see how I'll whip Frank!
Strip, Frank: I say, strip: don't you hear me, sir? Strip, Frank[!]
(Frank, crying & trembling, begins to unbutton his trousers.
Now, Francis, go down on the flogging-block. Hugh,
Take his shirt up behind. Very well: that will do.
    (Frank kneels down, & holds out his bottom for punishment.
See those scars! it's just three days, I think, since he got 'em.
And now; Master Francis, I'll tickle your bottom!
    (Flogs Frank. Frank roars for mercy. The other boys laugh.

No crying, sir, here! your offences are rank:
(Flogging him again.
Eh, Frank, my friend? How do you like it, friend Frank?
(Frank roars.
Some day, my fine fellow, you'll yet live to thank
(When you're older) the rod that is flogging you, Frank.
You've a brawny broad bottom to whip or to spank;
A bottom just made for the birch, my friend Frank.
The birch is a friend, boy, who never deserts you.
(Flogs Frank more & more severely.
Does it hurt you, eh, Frank? Yes, I see how it hurts you.
(Frank writhes with pain at each cut of the rod.
Keep quiet, sir — hold out your bottom, sir.
Frank (with a scream of agony as the birch fall again). Oh!
Please! Oh, sir! Oh, please, sir, don't punish me so!
I can't bear so much punishment!
Master (with a cut of the birch at every other word). Can't you, indeed,
Master Frank? You are here to be punished — to bleed
For your sins on the whipping-block, smarting with pain —
To be whipped — to be whipped — to be whipped, Master Fane!
To be whipped, Master Francis! (why else are you stripped?)
To be whipped, Master Frank! to be whipped! to be whipped!
(Frank roars.
Why, what does the youngster suppose that he's stripped for,
If not for a whipping? The faults that he's whipped for
Deserve a sharp taste of the birch: & the pain
That he suffers in sight of his playmates again
Ought to worn them from copying the faults of Frank Fane.

I can't say (**Swish! Swish!**) that I really expect
That correction (however severe) will correct
Such a boy as Frank Fane of his faults all at once —
Make Francis a scholar instead of a dunce —
A good boy instead of a bad boy; I wish
I could think so — could hope so: but other boys (**Swish!**)
Will take warning, I trust, by this sight, & refrain
From behaving as badly (**Swish! Swish!**) as Frank Fane,
Unless (**Swish! Swish! Swish! Swish! Swish! Swish!**)
they should wish
To be whipped with Frank Fane. (**Swish! Swish! Swish!**
Swish! Swish! Swish!)

Frank (roaring with pain). Oh! Oh, sir! oh, spare me for once, sir! Oh! Oh!
Oh, please, sir! You've flogged me so often, you know,
This half, sir, already! it hurts me, sir, so! (Sobbing bitterly.
It hurts me so awfully!

Master. That is the virtue
Of birch. Do you think I don't want, sir, to hurt you?
Do you think, when I strike, I don't mean to give pain —
Make you smart — make your bottom smart thoroughly, Fane?
At each cut on that naked & sensitive part
I am happy to see how I'm making you smart.
(Flogs Frank. Frank screams & cries & roars with the pain at each cut.
To-morrow you'll scarcely shirk school or miss church,
I fancy. — George Charlton, I want a fresh birch.

Frank. Oh, please, sir! Oh, please, not another, sir! please,
Not another fresh birch! Oh! — Oh! — Oh! (crying & sobbing.
George (offering the Master a couple of new green, sappy rods). Will not these
Do? I think, sir, you'll find them as lithe & as supple
As need be — as tough & as stinging a couple
Of rods as Frank Fane ever felt in his life.
Each touch of each twig in the course of the strife
Will sting like a wasp, sir, & cut like a knife
To the quick.
Master (with a smile). Ay, but, George, I asked only for one.
George. You'll want both, sir, I fancy, before you have done.
Master. Frank Fane, do you hear? You'll have Charlton to thank
If I lay a third rod on you presently, Frank.
(Frank sobs.
He knows you deserve, not the birch, but the cat —
The whip, sir! & so, Master Franky, take that!
(Flogs Frank. Frank roars with the pain.
Take that — & that, sir! You'll live to say 'thanky'
To the birch — to the birch & the whipping-block, Franky:
To the whipping-block, Fane, where so often you've knelt:
To the birch that your bottom so often has felt,
And so often has blushed to acknowledge as stronger
And tougher. (Flogs Frank more soundly than ever.
Frank (in tears). Oh! Oh, I can bear it no longer!

Oh, spare me, sir, please! I can't bear so much pain!
Oh! Oh! (The Master whips Frank till the blood runs down.

Master. I must think of your schoolfellows, Fane.
I must teach them a lesson. And then, you young dog,
You have really a beautiful bottom to flog.
A capital bottom for birching — as plump
As a peach. (He flogs Frank harder & harder at each stroke.

Frank (writhing in agony under the rod). Oh! Oh! Oh!

George (aside). Ah, the Doctor's a trump!
And he's right, Master Frank has a fine fleshy rump.
A stalwart stout broad pair of buttocks to tickle
Till the birch at each cut makes the ruddy drops trickle
From the smarting red skin that was lately so white,
From the writhing & tingling posteriors. He's right:
Frank Fane on the block is a beautiful sight:
Though the pain of each stroke makes him yelp like a dog,
Frank Fane's is a beautiful bottom to flog.

Master (holding the rod suspended over Frank). George!

George. Here, sir!

Master. Just bring me the flogging-roll here.

George. The flogging-roll, sir, for the half, or the year?

Master. For the half — & read out (Hush, you blubbering young oaf!)
(To Frank with a very severe cut of the birch)
How often Frank Fane has been hoisted this half.

George. Here's the list of his floggings this half: twenty-seven.

Master. And last half, I remember, he had but eleven:

Frank's Flogging

For I sent the account to his father, who wished
To be sure that his troublesome cub had been 'swished'
As soundly as ever a father could wish,
And as often. He wasn't half satisfied. (Swish!)
He said — (do you hear, you rebellious young dunce?)
That he thought a boy ought to be flogged at least once
Each morning, till cured of his idleness — healed
Of his naughtiness. Franky's backside was well wealed,
He allowed — you could see, when the youngster was stripped,
That Frank had been soundly & recently whipped!
The stripes were still red, & the cuts were still fresh,
On the naked expanse of his naughty boy's flesh:
On the naked expanse of his naughty boy's skin
There were signs that the birch-twigs had made the blood spin
And the flesh rise in ridges like [...] that swell:
Yes; Frank, he could see, had been flogged, & flogged well:
But, he thought, though the birch might be supple [& tough]
Frank had not been punished quite often enough[:]
Though the birch he had felt might be pliant & lithe
And the bottom that felt it might tingle & writhe
As no doubt Master Franky's posteriors had done,
Yet he wished that more birch had been spent on his son.
I approved him, & promised to do as he wished.
Now you know why Frank Fane is so often well 'swished'
As you call it: Sir Francis, his father, will thank
The birch that each morning does justice on Frank.

Each morning it shall, till the smart makes him know
How foolish it is to be wilfully slow
And provoke me — compel me — to punish him so.
(Flogging Frank again & again & again, very severely indeed.

Frank. Oh. Oh.

Master. Hold your tongue, my lad. (Flogging him again.

Frank. Please, sir! Oh. Oh.

Master. Hold your tongue, sir. I haven't half done with you: no.
(Flogs Frank again with all his strength.

Frank. Oh. Oh. I can't bear it. Oh. Oh, sir! Oh. Oh.
Oh. — Please, sir. — Oh. — Oh. — Oh. — Oh. — Oh, sir, I've had
Such a lot, sir. Oh. Oh. (Frank receives a fresh cut at each cry for mercy.

Master (with a very severe cut). Don't you like it, my lad?
You have only yourself, Master Francis, to thank.
You insist, as it were, on my flogging you Frank?
It's useless to howl & entreat & complain:
You leave me no choice but to punish you, Fane.
I'll teach you to wince at the sound of the word 'rod.'
(Looking at the rod with which has been whipping Frank.
You were right — very right, George: I <u>do</u> want a third rod.

Frank (writhing in agony on the flogging-block). Oh! Oh, sir! Oh, please, sir!

George (offering the Master a stout, supple, stinging birch). I thought so, sir.

Master (examining the twigs with an approving eye). Yes.
This will tickle Fane's bum for him well, I can guess.
The birch buds are as green & as thick as can be.
This will tickle Fane's bum pretty sharply, I see.
As yet it's not thoroughly flayed — only partly.
Yes — yes: this will tickle Fane's bum pretty smartly.

Frank’s Flogging. 5

Ay, this will draw blood — this will make the blood come:
Ay, these are the birch-twigs to tickle Fane’s bum.
Did you ever, my boy’s, see a rod that looked tougher
Or likelier, to make a young gentleman suffer —
Suffer pain at each cut — ay, & exquisite pain!
Don’t you think it will sting? won’t it hurt Master Fane?
You, Algernon Clavering, I think, ought to know
A good rod when you see it, & feel your skin glow,
Burn, tingle, & smart at the sight of it — eh?
Do you think, though I’ve punished you day after day,
And picked out the best rods I could possibly find
To attack you again & again from behind
Till you scarcely now flinch when you feel the rod fall, sir,
That you’d like to be whipped with this rod?
Algernon (laughing & wincing). Not at all, sir.
Master. I thought so. And you, Master Percy? you’ve had
Many tastes of the birch — your posteriors, my lad,
Have worn out not so many birch-rods — no, not quite —
As Algernon’s have: but, to give you your right,
You come next — do you think it an honour to come
Next Algernon, eh? is the blush on your bum
A blush, not of shame, but of pride, must we think[?]
Can you look on this rod in my hand, & not shrink?
(Percy flinches at sight of the birch, & claps both hands on his bottom.
Do you see, my lads — eh? did you see how he shrank?
— And now for a taste of the birch, Master Frank!

Ay — now for a taste of it! — Hold up his shirt,
(Flogs Frank.

Frank (roaring with the pain at each cut). Oh! — Oh!

Master. Ah, I thought so — I thought it would hurt.
Does it sting, sir — sting well? Does it scratch like a cat?
Does it bite like a bloodhound? Take that, sir — and that.
(Frank roars.
I'm ashamed of you, Frank; yes, I blush for you, Fane.
You should blush, my boy, deeper with shame than with pain
To behave like a baby: the shame should be crushing:
Your cheeks ought to blush as your bottom's blushing.
There's plenty of blood in your bottom to blush with
When we've got some tough birch-twigs to make the blood gush with.
I look on your blushing posteriors, & wish
I could see your face blush as your bottom has. Swish!
(Frank roars.
Tears & blood down your cheeks & posteriors are pouring
Are trickling & streaming — appealing, imploring
For mercy in vain, while Frank goes on roaring.
In vain, I say, Franky! — in vain, sir! — in vain!
When Frank leaves off crying & roaring with pain,
(**Swish!**) I (**Swish!**) will (**Swish!**) leave off flogging Frank Fane[!]
(Frank roars.
Swish!

Frank (screaming & roaring with pain at each fresh cut of the birch). Oh, sir!

Master. You [hear] how the lash makes him yelp,
My boys.

Frank (writhing with pain). Oh! Oh! Oh!

Master. Do you hear the young [whelp?]

Frank (sobbing). Oh, please, sir! oh, please, sir! oh, please, I can't help!
I can't help, sir! you hurt me so!
Master. Can't you, you whelp?
Take that! (Flogs Frank.
Algernon (aside). He don't howl as he takes it. Well done, Frank!
Master. That's better. I fancy you're tired of the fun, Frank.
If you take the next cut without crying, my lad,
That cut shall be really the last you'll have had
Nine times nine with the birch on your naked backside;
A good flogging — a real good sound flogging — I've tried,
(As you very well know, Master Frank) on your hide
A good many rods — aye, & good ones: no doubt,
Your posteriors have worn many scores of them out:
Many mornings in school, many noons after church,
Your naked posteriors have blushed from the birch:
Many evenings, before you went crying to bed,
Your smarting posteriors have felt it, and bled:
But never, I think, Mr. Fane, you'll allow,
Has your bottom been whipped more severely than now,
Let us see, though, before you get up, my good lad,
From the flogging-block, how many floggings you've had,
And how many cuts at each flogging, since last
You came back at the close of the holidays past.
But first (now you'd better not cry — as you know)
Take that, my boy! (Flogs Frank soundly. Frank roars. [81]

Frank (writhing under the lash). Oh, sir! Oh please, sir! Oh! Oh!
Master. You want a fresh dose, then? (Holding up the rod, & smiling.
Frank (trembling with fear, and flinching with pain). No, no, sir — oh no!
Master. I said, if you took this last cut like a man,
If I found you could bear it as many boys can,
No bigger or older than you, Master Fane,
I would let you get up from the flogging-block. Pain
As severe as you now most deservedly feel
Many others have felt, & will frequently kneel
Like you on the flogging-block, sentenced again
To feel it: but some of them bear it like men,
Without howling & writhing & crying for mercy
At each cut. Go and bring me the flogging-book, Percy —
The Black Book, I mean, of the school — which will tell
How often each boy has been flogged, & how well.
We shall find, when you read the particulars out,
That Frank has been often well flogged, I don't doubt,
Since he last came to school here again with the rest of you:
I'm aware that the name of the steadiest & best of you
Will be found more than once in the flogging-list — yes —
But not nearly as often as Fane's, I should guess.
— Read out now, George Charlton, the record you'll find
Of Fane's flagellations this half. Are you blind?
Can't you see where his name comes? it ought to be plain.
'Fane - Francis' — 'Fane - Francis,' & so forth: Frank Fane
Must be down on the list pretty often, I know.
George. Oh yes, sir — 'Fane, Francis; eighteen cuts.'

Master (giving Frank a sharp cut with the birch). Oho!
Eighteen — with two birches, I fancy — you've had
Rather more than eighteen cuts this morning, my lad.
Read on, George.
George (reading from the flogging-list). 'Fane, Francis: eighteen cuts.'
Master (giving Frank a smart cut on the bottom). Again?
You should have had three or four dozen, Frank Fane,
I feel sure.
George. 'Francis Fane; twenty-one cuts.'
Master. You see,
Francis Fane, that your name was beginning to be
Familiar, this half, to the registrar. Once,
'Fane, Francis,' the writer inscribed you, you dunce,
On the whipping-list; next 'Francis Fane' [takes the place]
Of 'Fane, Francis,' you see, on the scroll of disgrace
As your floggings grew frequenter. Next on the rank
of dishonour the name we shall see will be Frank.
And that name will be down, I expect, for some more cuts.
Swish! (Applying the birch to Frank's bottom with great severity.
Frank (writhing with pain). Oh, sir! oh, please, sir!
George. 'Frank Fane; twenty-four cuts.'
Master (giving Frank's bottom another lash). I thought so. (Frank roars.
George. 'Frank Fane; twenty-five cuts.'
(The Master again applies the rod to Frank's bottom.
Frank (roaring with pain). Oh! Oh!
George. Frank Fane; twenty-seven cuts.'
Master (giving Frank a very severe cut). And good ones, I know —

Like this one. (Frank writhes in agony on the flogging-block.
George. 'Frank Fane; thirty-six cuts. — Frank Fane' [7]
Master. Stop a minute. (Flogs Frank). Go on.
George. 'Thirty-six cuts, again.'
Master. Thirty-six again, eh? that was rather severe. (Flogs Frank. [8]
George. 'Frank Fane; forty-eight cuts.' A mark is set here — [9]
I don't know what it means, sir.
Master. Indeed, let me look.
Wait a minute, though, Charlton. (Flogs Frank.) Now give me the book.
Hold the rod for me, Algernon Clavering, Ah, yes, ~~10~~
I know what it means, or at least I can guess.
It means that a boy must in future be reckoned
In the first class, I think, of black sheep — not the second —
And must never thence forward — no, never again —
Get off easily; never be spared now & then,
As a boy sometimes is who is usually steady.
Have I ever spared Algy, or Redgie, or Freddy;
Or Wilfred, or Edwin, or Leonard, or Percy,
Or Edward, or Arthur, when pleading for mercy?
All these are enrolled in the scapegraces' rank:
But few have been punished much oftener than Frank.
Take the flogging-book back, George, & put it away
In its place.
George. Oh, but, please, sir —
Master. What now, my boy — eh?
George. I thought, sir, you told me to read out the list
Of his floggings this half; but if <u>you</u> don't insist —
Master. Go on, my boy — yes — you're quite right; yes, I do, boys.
It's wholesome for Frank, & it's useful for you boys.

Frank's Flogging

8

18 cuts to come

George. "Frank Fane; twenty-five cuts.'
Master. Take that, sir. (Flogs Frank.) Go on,
George Charlton.
George. 'Frank-Fane; twenty-four cuts.'
Master. We've gone
Some way through the half by this time, eh?
George. O, no, sir
Three weeks & two days.
Master. Then take that, Frank. (Flogs Frank.
Frank (with a fresh burst of tears). Oh! Oh, sir!
Master. Oh, oh, sir, indeed! You young rascal! the pain
Of a flogging should be so familiar, Frank Fane,
To the reddening posteriors that redden once more
From the strokes of the birch that has left them so sore
So often, that we, sir, who hear how you roar
And see how you cry, are surprised, my good lad,
That in spite of the many sound whippings you've had
This year, & last year, & the year before that,
You should yelp like a puppy & squeal like a cat
When the birch you deserve to feel daily, you dunce,
Is duly applied to your bottom for once,
And a dozen good floggings you've managed to shun
Are combined & compressed into one.
George. 'Frank Fane: forty-eight cuts.'
Master (raising the rod). Four dozen cuts, eh?

He'll have had, I'm afraid, twice as many today.
His record is red: his offences are rank:
Hold your bottom out, sirrah! (Flogging him.) Take that, Mr. Frank! 12
(Frank roars.

George. 'Frank Fane: thirty-six cuts.'

Master (with a very severe cut of the birch). And all this in vain! 13
(Frank roars.
All this flogging, it seems, thrown away on Frank Fane!
All this birch almost wasted!

George. 'Frank Fane' — here's a blot, sir:
Twenty-four cuts, I think — twenty-four, is it not sir?

Master. Twenty-four? no, my boy — twenty-seven (Flogs Frank.) Go ahead. 14
He ought to have had thirty-six cuts instead. (Frank roars.

George. 'Frank Fane: sixty-three cuts.'

Master (flogging him severely). Oh, oh, Master Frank! 15
(Frank roars.
That was something like punishment – eh, sir?

Arthur (aside to Reginald). He shrank,
— Did you see? — poor old chap, at the thought of it.

Reginald. Yes:
He'll get something to shrink for next time, I should guess.

George. 'Frank Fane: twenty-one cuts.'

Master. Take that, sir. (Flogs Frank.) Go on, George. 16
(Frank roars.
Hold your tongue, Frank! — Why, where are the wits of you gone, George?
Wool-gathering?

George. O no, sir — I just lost the place
For a minute.

Frank's Flogging.

9

[…] cuts to come

Master (smiling). The sight of a friend in disgrace
Was too much for your feelings, perhaps? & the pain
That you felt, I presume, at the thought how young Fane
must have suffered when under the rod, was so keen
That you couldn't go on, but broke down — just between
Seventeen — that's the number, I think, & eighteen —
The next number, unless I'm mistaken, to come
In the list of the whippings this half that your chum
has incurred? Did compassion & grief strike you dumb
At the sorrowful sight of his blushing bare bum?
Did the cuts make you wince as your schoolfellow got 'em,
At the pitiful sight of his bloody bare bottom?
George. Not exactly, sir: no.
Master. Then go on, sir.
George (reading from the flogging-book). 'Frank Fane:
Forty-eight cuts.' 17
Master. With two or three birches. It's plain
Frank doesn't much mind or much care for the pain.
Take that, sir! (Flogs Frank.
Frank (roaring & writhing in agony under the rod). Oh! Oh!
Willie (aside). He don't mind it — oh no!
Not at all! How the blood runs afresh at each blow!
George. 'Frank Fane: twenty-five cuts.' (The Master flogs Frank. 18
Frank (crying bitterly). Oh, please, sir! Oh! Oh!
Oh, I'll try to do better, — I will, sir, indeed!
Master. How often next time did the birch make you bleed —

Can you guess, my lad — eh?
Frank (crying & sobbing). I don't know! I can't guess!
George. 'Frank Fane: twenty-seven cuts.'
Master. Ay, ay, my lad — yes — 19
(Flogs Frank.
I seem to remember that flogging; don't you?
(Frank roars.
And I think you'll remember this flogging, sir, too.
George. 'Frank Fane: thirty-six cuts.' 20
Master. Take that! (Flogs Frank.
Percy (aside). What a spree!
(Frank roars.
George. 'Frank Fane: sixty-three cuts.' 7 cuts to [come]
Master. Again sixty-three? 21
Why, clearly, then, seven times nine is the sum
That the birch must work out on Frank Fane's naked bum
Each time he presents it by way of a slate
To be written or ciphered on. (Flogs Frank. Frank roars.
Frank (writhing in torture under the birch). Oh!
Master. It's too late,
Master Frank, to cry out when you've been whipped: it's in vain;
And your bottom must surely be used to the pain;
For you're pretty well used to the birch, Master Fane.
There are only five boys, I believe, in the school
Who have oftener been flogged.
George (with the confidence of a conscious favourite). Not this half, sir: but who'll
Undertake to determine how often last half
Teddy Collingwood smarted? it makes a chap laugh
To think of it.
Master (smiling). Yes, Master George — so I see, sir
George. And others too smarted as often as he, sir.

Fred Norton, I think, was flogged oftener still:
And Fred wasn't oftener flogged, sir, than Will:
And Edwin was constantly whipped, sir — for cheek:
And Leonard was whipped three or four times a week.
Leonard (aside). Don't I wish I could lick him!
Edwin (aside). The liar!
Fred (aside, clenching his fists, & reddening with passion). The sneak!
Willie If I could but whip Charlton, O, wouldn't he squeak!
Frank (aside). It's too bad! it's too beastly unfair — yes, it is —
To give any chap half such a flogging as this!
To keep a chap waiting, and smarting like fun,
Between the last cut & the next, when each one
Seems harder, & sharper, & harder to bear,
Than the last! but, by Jove, though, I wouldn't much [care,]
If I could but see Charlton to-morrow kneel down
On the block, with his shirt up: I shan't, though: the frown
That condemns me & Algie & Redgie & Percy
And Willie & Fred to be whipped without mercy
Has never made Charlton feel queer — hardly ever,
At least — the mean beast is so awfully clever!
If Birkenshaw frowns on his theme or his sum
And the birch would belabour another chap's bum,
There's always some sneaking excuse for it — O,
If I were but grown up! I'd not thrash him — oh no!
Master. Frank seems to be weary of waiting — to wish
That his flogging was over, I think, my boys? Swish!
Swish! (giving Frank two very severe cuts on the bottom.

Frank (sobbing bitterly). Oh! [... cuts]
Master. Now, my boys, only look at him: see [to come]
How he likes what a boy as unruly as he
Is certain to get — most deservedly. You
Have been whipped pretty often this half, I think, Hugh —
Eh?
Hugh. Only thirteen times, sir.
Master. *Only* thirteen?
Well, others, no doubt, have been oftener seen
On the flogging-block, Hughie: I heartily wish
That the sight you see now may be good for you. Swish!
(Flogs Frank soundly. Frank roars with pain. 24
Read on, Master George: you're not yet, I'm afraid,
At the end of the list: the two last cuts I've laid
On Franky's posteriors have simply anticipated
The record: read on, that all doubts may be dissipated.
George (reading). 'Frank Fane: twenty-four cuts. Frank Fane: twenty-four cuts.
Frank Fane: twenty-seven cuts.'
Master (raising the rod). You've had a few more cuts
To-day, Master Francis. Take that, my lad! (Flogs Frank.
Frank (writhing & cowering under the lash). Oh!
Oh please, sir!
George (reading). 'Frank Fane: forty-eight cuts.'
Master. So! so!
That's better: eh, Franky, my boy? Forty-eight cuts!
No wonder your bottom bears signs of the late cuts
It smarted so sharply from. (Flogs Frank. Frank sobs & writhes.
Frank (looking up with streaming eyes). Please, sir!
George (reading). 'Frank Fane:
Thirty-nine cuts:' for larking with Redgie Loraine
Out of bounds, you remember, last week, sir.
Master (raising his rod for a very severe stroke at parting). I do:
And Redgie and Frank must remember it too. (Flogs Frank. Frank roars.
Get up, Master Frank. (Frank, crying bitterly, gets up from the flogging-block.) You don't like so much pain[?]
Then mind you keep clear of the flogging-block, Fane. [...]

On the public flogging-block
Frank was whipped at twelve o'clock:
For doing what Frank should not have done,
Frank was whipped again at one:
For not doing what he had to do,
Frank was whipped again at two:
With all the school drawn up to see,
Frank was whipped again at three;
While his bottom still was sore,
Frank was whipped again at four;
Still to keep the smart alive,
Frank was whipped again at five;
Next, for all his naughty tricks,
Frank was whipped again at six;

The Flogging-Block. Eclogue VIII. Philip's Flogging.

Part I.

Scene, the private flogging-room. Enter Edward and Philip.

Edward. You'll catch it to-day, I can tell you, Phil Dil!
Your bottom will get it as hot, Master Phil,
As the birch-twigs can give you, Philip — it will!
Philip. I don't care — I've been flogged three or four times already
This half; I don't mind — I don't care for it, Teddy.
Edward. Oh! don't you, indeed, Master Philip? By God,
What a lark! here's the latest recruit of the rod,
Still smarting from yesterday's punishment, come
To see what the birch has to say to your bum.

Enter Frank.

How's your bottom, Frank Fane? How's your bottom to-day?
Is it sore? does it smart? How's your bottom, sir, eh?
Frank (laughing & wincing). Get out, you great fool!
Edward (giving Frank a sharp smack on the bottom). Do you want a good spank?
Frank (writhing with pain). Don't! Damn you! I say!
Edward. Look at Philip now, Frank.
He doesn't — he says that he doesn't, by God! —
Care a bit for a flogging: he laughs at the rod.
He'll bear it, you'll see, without wincing — he will!
We shall see.
Frank. Don't let Collingwood bully you, Phil.
Don't mind him.
Philip (laughing). I don't: though he chaffs a chap so,
He's a jolly good fellow at bottom, I know.
Frank. At bottom? His bottom's a jolly good field
For the birch — it's all bloody & ridgy & wealed

Since the day before yesterday, wasn't it, Ned?
When your naked backside for the hundredth time bled,
When your bloody backside for the hundredth time smarted,
And the ruddy big drops at each lash on it started,
And trickled all over your bottom — eh, cousin?

Edward (sulkily). 'Twasn't I who got yesterday, was it? nine dozen,
Nine dozen good lashes, & howled with the pain,
And blubbered & roared out for mercy in vain:
The name of the fellow who did is Frank Fane.

Frank. No, it doesn't take nine — no, nor six, nor three dozen,
To make you sing out on the whipping-block, cousin.
you cry while you're taking your breeches down, Teddy,
And when first the rod strikes you you're whimpering already.
I'll bet you Phil Dilston will bear it — he will,
I'll bet you — much better. Eh! won't you now, Phil?

Philip. I'll try — I don't know, Frank.

Edward. You won't, then, Phil Dil?
Old Birkenshaw means, sir, to give you your fill,
I can tell you — he said so to Charlton, I know —
And Charlton said 'Yes, sir; pray do, sir;' & so
You're in for a jolly good flogging, by God,
Master Philip — a rather sharp taste of the rod.
You needn't frown, redden, & clench your right fist: I'm
Quite sure you'll be flogged, Phil, most awfully this time.
You'll be flogged as you've never been flogged, my boy, yet,
You'll get a fine bloody whipped bottom, I'll bet.
I'll bet you old Birkie will give it you, Phil,
As hard as he ever has given it — he will!

Philip's Flogging.

Philip. O, Frank, do you think — are you sure that he will?
I was flogged, you know, awfully last time!
Frank. Well, Phil,
I don't know — how the devil can any chap tell?
But I fancy he'll make your whipped bottom smart well.
You'd better just make up your mind to it. Here
They come!
Edward. And the victim is trembling with fear.
Just look how he shrinks — & each eye has a tear.
Phil Dilston! Phil Dilston 'your penance draws near.'

Enter the Master, preceded by George, who carries a stout, supple, & well-budded birch rod: Algernon, Frederick, Edward, Wilfred, Leonard, Reginald, Arthur, Edwin, & Percy.

Master. Philip Dilston, make ready for punishment.
(Philip with trembling hands, begins to unbutton his trousers.
Willie (aside). Come!
For once we shall see Master Philip's bare bum!
Edward (aside). I've seen it, Will, three times — no, four times — this half.
Willie (aside). Why, I thought he had never been flogged!
Edward. That's all chaff.
He's not such a novice in flogging — not he
Though he never was whipped as he's going to be.
Willie. Eh? How do you know?
Edward. Never mind, Will — I do.
He'll be flogged like Frank Fane, or like me, or like you,
Or like Algernon Clavering or Redgie Loraine.
Master. Come here; you must hold Philip's shirt up, Frank Fane.

Go down, Philip Dilston, this instant, sir — down —
Take him down! the rebellious young rascal!

Arthur (aside to Reginald). That frown
Means mischief. Poor Phil! what a swishing he'll get!
Such a jolly good swishing he never had yet.

Reginald. It's time that he did, then — he isn't the best of us —
And he ought to be jolly well swished — like the rest of us.
(George and Percy lay hold of Philip by the shoulders & arm, and force him down, struggling & crying, on the block. Frank takes his shirt up, while the two bigger boys hold him down. The Master, who has taken the rod from George before he laid hands on Philip, begins operations by three severe cuts on Philip's naked bottom.

Philip (sobbing bitterly). Oh! — Oh, sir! — Oh, please!

Master. Why, he's crying already!
And we thought he was going to take it like Freddy —
Like that impudent rascal Fred Norton there. Swish[!]
It may be his ambition to do so — his wish
To behave under punishment (Swish!) like a lad
Who can bear any number of cuts he has had
Without crying — can take a sharp lash like a fillip —
But (**Swish!**) you can't stand it all, I see, Philip.
(**Swish!**)

Philip (crying & writhing). Oh, sir!

Master (whipping him again). This chubby-cheeked plump little bum
Must expect a good number of lashes to come.

(Swish!) Yes, if your bum's not as hard as a mill-stone,
I'll (**Swish!**) make it smart through & through, Master Dilston.
Swish! Swish! (Whipping Philip's bottom soundly.

Philip (crying bitterly). Oh! Oh! Oh, sir! Oh, please, sir! Oh! Oh!
Oh, please let me off, sir! it hurts me, sir, so!
Oh, I'll try to do better, sir! Spare me, sir!

Master (laying on the lash with all his might). **No!**
Swish! That makes thirteen, Master Dilston, I think[!]

Edwin (aside to Leonard). What a cut was that last one! the sight makes me wink.
And it took Philip's breath away — left him, by God,
No breath to cry out with. (Philip is heard sobbing bitterly.

Master (laying down the well-worn birch). George, bring me a rod:
And mind that the twigs & the buds are all fresh.
Master Dilston must suffer today in the flesh.

George (handing him a fresh rod). I think this will hurt, sir.

Master (examining the well-budded twigs with a smile). I'm certain it will.
Take that, Master Dilston! — take that, Master Phil!
Take that, sir! and that! Does it hurt you, Phil Dil?
Eh? (**Swish!**) does it hurt you, or doesn't it, Phil?
Swish! Swish! (Flogging Philip's bottom without mercy.

Philip (writhing under the torture). I can't bear it! Oh, please, sir, I can't!
Oh! Oh!

Master. Would you like to get up, sir? You shan't
Just yet. Hold him fast now, my boys — hold him down.
Swish! (Whips Philip with the utmost strength of his arm.

Philip (in agony, writhing under the rod at each lash). Oh, sir!

Master (whipping him severely). Take that, sir, for larking up town.

Philip. O, please, I was fagging, sir, please, sir; I won't
Ever do it again. Oh! Oh! Oh, sir! Oh, don't,
Don't, please! I was fagging — they fagged me up town:
It wasn't my fault.

George (aside). But your breeches are down,
All the same, Master Philip. Ha, ha! does it hurt?
Ah, I know how you wish you could pull down your shirt!

(The Master whips Philip's bottom till the blood runs at each cut.

Philip (crying & roaring with the pain). Oh, please, sir, it wasn't my fault, sir!

Master (giving Philip's bottom a very severe cut). Whose was it, then?
If the secret is safe in your private deposit, then
A good sound public flogging to-morrow must do
Full justice on him — or on them — & on you.
I whip you today for your personal offence;
But, (**Swish!**) as it seems — if I gather your sense —
That another or others were guiltier than you,
I'll whip you severely to-morrow, in view
Of the whole upper school — not in sight of a few,
As now: you shall smart for the whole of the crew —
Not alone for yourself — for the other boys too.
When you should be in school, but are loitering & lagging,
It's no sort of excuse, sir, to say that you were fagging.
I no nothing of that: but I know, Master Phil,
That I ought to chastise you, my lad — & I will.

Philip (crying). Oh! Oh, sir! You know, sir, a fellow must go
If he's fagged — he can't help — he can't help it, sir! Oh!

Philip's Flogging.

Master (whipping Philip smartly). Can't help it, sir? What do you
mean by 'can't help'?
Do you mean to provoke me, you impudent whelp?
Swish! — Swish!
Philip (writhing with agony). Oh! Oh, please, sir! Oh, please, sir, you know,
If a lower boy's fagged out of bounds, he must go!
Oh, please, sir! please, please, sir! I begged, sir, & prayed
To get off — but they wouldn't — I knew I'd get flayed —
I said so — I begged & I prayed to be let off
That errand — but, please, sir, I couldn't, sir, get off!
I had, sir, to go — they compelled me by kicking —
If I hadn't, you know, I'd have got such a licking!
They'd have almost half killed me! Oh! Oh! (sobbing.
Master (whipping Phillip so hard as to break the twigs). So, I see
There are others you fear in the school more than me.
There are higher authorities, are there? than mine.
I meant, sir, to give you just seven times nine —
Twenty-seven to begin with today — to your sorrow —
And then, my good lad, thirty-six cuts tomorrow.
But now I shall give you, though only a small boy,
In doses of nine — eighty-one cuts in all, boy.
It will do you no harm — that's the birch's great virtue
But I think, Philip Dilston, you'll find it will hurt you.
Philip (crying bitterly). Oh, please, it'll kill me, sir! Oh, sir, it will!
Oh! Please, sir! Oh! Oh, sir! Oh!
Arthur (aside). Poor little Phil!
Master. Come, sir, don't be a coward as well as a dunce.
Philip. Oh, please let me have it, sir, please, all at once!

I'll try, sir, to bear it — to bear it today —
But don't, sir, don't whip me tomorrow, sir, pray!
Don't whip me again, sir! don't whip me again!
I shall hardly be able to bear it, sir, then.
I'll try not to cry, sir; I'll try not to cry;
I shall hardly be able to help; but I'll try;
I will, sir — please, please, sir, I will, sir, indeed!

George (aside). O, by Jove, how the birch makes him blubber and bleed!

Master. Come, how many cuts do you think you have had
Already — eh, Philip? How many, my lad?
How many? Eh, Dilston? (Flogs him again: he roars.

Philip (writhing under the birch). Oh! Oh, I can't tell!

Master. I see I must whip your bare bum for you well:
I see I must whip your backside, Master Phil,
Pretty smartly — I see that I must: and I will.
(Flogs Philip again & again. Philip roars with pain.

Edward (aside). By Jove, though, he's catching it nicely today!

Master. How many cuts now has he had, should you say,
George Charlton? I think about thirty cuts — eh?

George. Five more, sir I think: I feel sure of it: I've
Kept an eye on him, sir — & I think thirty-five.
Ever since, sir, you first laid the lash on him, I've
Kept an eye on his bottom. He's had thirty-five.

Master. I can trust you, I know, to speak truth — or be dumb.
And I saw you were keeping an eye on his bum.
It's pretty well wealed, & decidedly sore:
So today it shall only have just one cut more.
There are, then, forty-five cuts tomorrow to come:
Thirty-six cuts today are enough for his bum.
(He gives Philip's bottom a very severe cut of the birch.
Get up — get away, sir: you know, to your sorrow,
I shall give your backside forty-five cuts tomorrow.
(Philip gets up from the flogging-block, roaring with pain, and exit.

Philip's Flogging. 5

Part II

Scene, the public flogging-room. Enter George, dragging in Philip by the collar.

George. Come on, sir! come in, sir! (He gives Philip a cuff on the head & a kick on the bottom.
Philip. Please, Charlton, don't kick me!
My bottom's so tender! I know you can lick me
Smack my face — box my ears — punch my head — pull my hair.
But, please, I'm so sore, I can't bear it just there!
George. You can't bear it? I'll try what your bottom can bear.
(George pinches Philip's bottom all over, & then smacks it.
Philip (wincing & crying). Oh! Oh! It's a shame! Oh, you know it's so sore!
George. And I know you're just going to get a lot more.
Talk of yesterday's swishing! you'll find that your bum
Doesn't know what a flogging is yet. Here they come!

Enter the Master, rod in had; Algernon, Percy, Reginald, Edward, Frank, Willie, Edwin, Arthur, Leonard, Frederick, Rupert, Hugh, Walter, & Bertram.

Master. Philip Dilston!
George (aside to Philip). Look out, my boy!
Philip (in a trembling voice). Here, sir.
George (aside to Philip). He's fiercer
To look at than usual. Speak up, you fool!
Philip. Here, sir.
Master. Take your trousers down.
Philip. Please, sir! Oh, please, sir, I had
Such a lot of it yesterday, please, sir!
Master (giving Philip a cut on the head with the rod). My lad,
You must learn that obedience alone is the rule
Prompt, instant obedience, my boy — for the school
And each boy in it.
George (aside to Philip). Down with your breeches, you fool!

For each minute you'll get a cut extra — you will —
For each minute you keep us all waiting, Phil Dil.

Philip (looking at the Master with tears in his eyes). Please, please, let me off, sir!

Master. No, no, Master Phil:
Take your trousers down.

Philip. Yes, sir — yes, please, sir, I will.

Master. Go down. Arthur Clifford, you'll hold up his shirt.
Now look at this rod — should you say it would hurt?
Eh, Dilston? speak up, my boy.

Philip (pausing in the process of unbuttoning his trousers). Yes, sir.

Master (raising the rod to deliver the first cut). It will,
Or I'm greatly mistaken.

(Philip lets down his trousers, & kneels. Arthur pulls up his shirt.

Take that, Master Phil!

(Flogs Philip.

Does it hurt you as much as you thought it would hurt you?
Obedience, my boy, is a youngster's first virtue,
And the second is industry. You Master Phil,
Have to learn them, as I have to teach — & I will.

(Flogs Philip.

Philip (writhing with pain). Please! Oh, sir! Oh, please! I can't bear it today!
Oh, sir! please let me off, sir! Oh, do, sir! Pray, pray
Pray, pray let me off! Oh, sir, do! Oh! Oh! Oh!
Oh, do let me off, sir! it hurts me, sir, so!
It hurts me so awfully! Please, sir! Oh, please, sir!
Oh! Oh!

Master (with a good hard cut of the birch). When I see a small boy on his knees, sir,
With his breeches down, (**Swish!**) I'm accustomed to hear —
I expect it — such cries as now ring in my ear.
You shall find that a flogging is something to fear.

Philip's Flogging.

Where's the new boy? Come here, Master Bertram. Have you
Ever seen a boy flogged till today — when you do,
I should say, see what's meant by a flogging?

Bertram (grinning at the recollection). Yes, please, sir.
I've only seen one fellow down on his knees, sir,
With his breeches down, ever — before I came here.
But I've seen him swished often & often.

Master. I fear
The sight has not made the impression it should
Have made on you, Bellingham. Would you, sir — would
You like, if your conduct, sir, hadn't been good,
To kneel down where Phil Dilston — your form-fellow — kneels?

Bertram. No, please, sir.

Master (smiling). The boy you saw whipped — were his weals
As thick and as red as Phil Dilston's — as ruddy
And as ridgy?

Bertram. Oh yes, sir; his bum was all bloody.

Master. And what was his name?

Bertram. Redgie Swinburne, sir.

Master. Oh!
I've heard that youngster before. So you know
That fellow?

Bertram. Oh, yes — he's my cousin, sir.

Master. So!
I perceive that the Cliffords & Bellinghams come
Of a stock in which all boys — not one boy, or some
Here & there, but all boys of all houses akin to it, —
If they see any mischief, go plunging right into it.

Else surely they would not, with all of their cousins,
Count their stripes by the score & their floggings by dozens.
And this youngster, Phil Dilston, who's catching it hot now,
Is a Kinsman of theirs & of yours — is he not, now?

Bertram. Yes, please, sir.

Master. Well, now you shall see, sir, please God,
Whether Philip will profit or not by the rod.
You shall see — we shall all see it proved on the spot —
Whether Dilston can bear a good whipping or not.
Now, Dilston, sir, hold out your bottom: I wish
You to feel the full smart of each lash on it. Swish!

(Applying the birch to Philip's bottom with all his strength.

Philip. Oh! Please, sir, I'll never — Oh! Oh, I can't bear it
Any longer! My bottom's so tender, sir! Spare it!
Oh, if you must whip me, don't whip me just there — it
Does hurt so! Oh! Oh, sir! Oh! Oh! I can't bear it!
Oh, I will be a good boy — I'll try to be good!
O, I can't, sir, help crying — I would if I could!

Master. I don't care my boy, whether you can or you can't —
(Swish! Swish!) but escape it — avoid it — you shan't.
You have seen me quite recently whipping the tallest boys
In the school as I whipped them when they were the smallest boys;
And small boys like you must not hope — should not wish —
To escape what their elders have suffered from. Swish!
Swish! Swish!

Philip (in tears). Oh! Oh! Oh!

Master. Does it hurt you, my lad?
Swish! Swish! is the pain (swish, swish, swish!) very bad?
The more a boy smarts at your age, Master Phil,
The better it is for him. Silence! be still!

Frederick's Flogging

Make ready, make ready the birch for Freddy!
    Once more, once more have we caught him [tripping];
And you, Master Freddy, my boy, make ready —
    Make ready, my boy, for a good sound whipping!
Here's the flogging-block ready prepared for you, Freddy;
    You fought with Harry — with Frank you quarrelled;
You know your way to the flogging-block, eh?
    You should know it if any boy does, Fred Thorold.
You have climbed, swam, & ridden in places forbidden;
    You played truant with Edward to bathe on the
                the Witches' Down;
So take down your breeches! — You did, my boy — which is
    The cause why today you must needs take your
                breeches down.
You knew the rules, Freddy my boy — so did Teddy:
    Don't answer me, Fred[,] don't pretend you forgot 'em!
You both knew the rule & the law of the school;
    Here's a birch — here's a birch — here's a birch for your bottom!
I've whipped you already a dozen times, Freddy,
    In sight of your juniors in age & superiors,
Since you came back to school here, for playing
                the fool here;
    Here's a stinging birch rod for your smarting posteriors!

Though your bottom were tougher, I'd still make it suffer —
    Though your bottom were frozen, I'd soon make it glow;
I won't spare you one single smart cut; don't it tingle
    Already? yes, Freddy, you're tingling, I know.
There's a case to be tried here on Frederic's backside here,
    On a criminal charge — of misconduct in church:
Though his bottom were tougher, his bottom should suffer —
    His bottom should suffer the tortures of birch!
Nine rods, had I got 'em, should brush his bare bottom —
    Should brush his bare bottom — should make his bum blush,
Should leave his bum blushing & red from its brushing;
    'Tis a jolly stout brawny broad bottom to brush.
I must whip Master Fred's bum still harder than Ted's bum;
    I must teach you, Fred Thorold, to shrink at my rod;
Though you bottom were tougher than steel, it should suffer —
    It should suffer the smart of the strokes of the rod.
After twelve I'll whip Ted's bum; but first I'll whip Fred's bum;
    Take your breeches down instantly, sir, & make ready;
There's a birch too for Teddy's bum even as for Freddy's bum;
    But the first & the best rod I've kept for you, Freddy.
— So the schoolmaster speaks; & the schoolboy's red cheeks
    Grow pale at each word of his lawful superiors;
— 'Not a word, sir!' he screeches: 'Boy, take down your breeches!'
    And Frederick discovers his naked posteriors.
By the long crimson streaks on those brawny round cheeks
    We can guess how he smarted & writhed when he got 'em;
By the look of those weals we can guess how he feels
    While he waits for a taste of the birch on his bottom.

Edgar's Flogging

O blushing Muse of birch, who [...] we [bow]
    To chant the torture of the twigs that sting,
What sufferer shall our song make famous now?
    Of what boy's bottom shall we choose to sing!
I can scarce choose among all these; do thou
    Pick out some new boy fit for bum brushing.
I see one stand out blushing red as dawn;
I know the bright dark eyes of Edgar Vaughn.

'You boy, have you been ever flogged before?'
    So, birch in hand, the master smiling speaks,
And looks the last week's list of flogged boys o'er,
    But no such name is down these many weeks.
'Yes, please sir, I've been three times flogged — no more,'
    Poor Edgar stammers out with burning cheeks.
'I'm glad at least you haven't told a lie.
Well — we'll make up for lost time by & by.

'Take down your breeches.' Edgar hears, & feels
    His hands grow clammy to the finger-tips
And his young heart stop beating, as he kneels
    And his face blanches to the quivering lips,
And his white bottom, innocent of weals,
    Tingles, & all the flesh between his hips,
Still smooth & snowy as a baby's bum,
Winces with fearful sense of strokes to come

And Charlie Collingwood & Redgie Fane
    Hold Edgar's shirt up — half amused, & half

Edgar's Flogging.

Compassionate, though pity here were vain,
    And Edgar stands in fear of Charlie's chaff;
For often, smarting still & flushed with pain,
    He has heard him jest at his own scars & laugh,
Take off the doctor's ways & words, & mock
The next boy writhing on the flogging-block.

A stout broad-shouldered brown-haired bright-eyed youth,
    With plump round ruddy cheeks & sturdy neck.
With strong & [sunburnt] hands & laughing mouth,
    As red as berries that the wild birds peck,
'Tis strange he was not oftener flogged, in sooth,
    ['Tis strange] that his bare bum [showed] no seam or fleck,
No sanguine sign or imprint of the rod;
His innocence of skin was surely odd.

You'd say the lad was just the kind of fellow
    Cut out for birching; just the boy to feel
Birch [twice] a day, & writhe & cry & bellow,
    Sob at each stroke & weep for [...] weal:
Soft skinned, broad-bottomed ripe for birch as [...]
    Fruit for the hand of truant boys to steal:
Yet Edgar had been flogged but three times; see
The great white bum where many [weals] must be!

For with a grin the master, strong of arm,
    Runs high the pliant birch-twigs tough & tight
(The swishing sound thrills Edgar with alarm)
    And after [some] dread pause with all his might
Strikes Edgar's naked bottom; soon the warm
    Red ridges, thick & throbbing, [stand] to sight;
Again the birch gives Edgar's bum a blow;
Again; & all the roof echoes 'Oh!'

And a fourth stinging stroke makes Edgar cry
    Louder; & with his eye the master [singling]

(Edgar's Flogging).

2)

A sensitive & tender part to try,
 Where burning red & natural white are mingling,
Strikes & so hard he makes the birch-twigs fly;
 And Edgar feels his naked bottom tingling
Even to the very bone; & twig & bud
Blush with the first big drops of Edgar's blood.

Ay, look at Edgar's bottom! You boys there,
 This was the boy, you recollect, who said
He didn't fear the rod — he didn't care —
 Not he! you'd never see his bottom red —
And now the whole school sees his bottom bare,
 What colour is it? Ay, boy, hide your head.
Bow down your stubborn neck & hide your face —
You cannot hide the part in most disgrace —

You cannot hide your bottom, Edgar! No —
 There are the proofs, my boy! the signs that tell
Your state & fate, the characters that shew
 If Edgar Vaughan has not been flogged right well
Flogged till each fresh cut makes him cry out 'Oh!'
 Flogged till the bloody ridges smart & swell —
Flogged till he writhes all over as he kneels —
Flogged till his bottom is one mass of weals.

'[Oh, please, sir …, sir!'] How the whipped boy cries
 And sobs each time his […]
[…] master turns imploring eyes
 As toward the shrine of an avenging god
The bright red stripes on Edgar's […] thighs
 Are [spangled] with great crimson flakes of blood;
His bottom blushes like a […]
'[…] does it sting, eh? does it hurt you, Vaughan?'

Edgar's Flogging

'Take that, sir! that — & that — & that — & that!
No crying here, sir! hold your tongue, I say!
There — swish — swish — swish — swish —spat, spat, spat, spat, spat!
It makes you wince — it makes you smart sir, eh?
I'll have no crying here in school, that's [flat] —
Swish! you were — swish — complained of yesterday —
Hold up Vaughan's shirt! let's see the boy's white back —
So! swish — swish — swish — swish — swish — swish — smack, smack, smack, smack!

'Well, Vaughan, how d'you like it, boy! it stings
[...] little? Does it hurt, sir — hurt?
You've been complained of — swish — for [various] things
And — swish! — I'll [...] you — swish! — full [deserve]
Don't cry, sir! I don't like a boys that [...] —
I would [...]
Nay, then you [...]
'Oh please, sir!' Swish! 'Oh!' Swish! Swish! Swish! Swish! 'Oh, sir!'

Swish! 'Oh, sir, how it stings! Oh, dear sir! Whish!
'Oh, sir, I'll never, please, sir, talk in church —
Oh, please, sir, I'll do all, sir, all you wish[!]'
The whipped boy wriggles like a landed [perch] —
'But oh, sir, let me off, sir, [...], sir! Swish!
'Oh, dear sir, oh, sir, please, put down the birch!
You know I've not been often flogged before
Oh, don't, don't, don't, don't flog me any more!

[Oh], sir! Oh! Oh! I can't — can't — can't — can't bear it!
You hit so hard, sir — please, sir, not so hard!'

Edgar's Flogging

Swish! 'Silence, sir! a boy of any spirit
    Would be ashamed of whining afterward.
The rod was not put in my hand to spare it
    But — swish — to leave the truant's bottom scarred.'
'Oh, don't hit there, sir — any place but that!'
Swish — swish — swish — swish — swish! spat — spat — spat — spat — spat!

'So, there it hurts you! eh, sir? there you are sore!
    It stings you there, sir, does it? eh, sir, eh?'
As each fresh cut elicits a fresh [roar]
    From Edgar — 'Stop that crying, sir, [Stop]!
It hurts you, does it, [eh?] well, we'll hurt you more.
    So that's the place, [then], is it? [...]
To hurt you, is it. ['Tis] the birch's [...]
To hurt boys — yes, to hurt them [—] yes, to hurt you.

'Eh, does it hurt, sir, does it hurt [...]
    Did that cut hurt you, [Edgar ...]
Don't hit that place again, sir! I can't bear
    The pain. I can't[,] sir! [...]
I'm sorry for you — but it's only fair
    That you should smart like other boys, [...]
'Oh, please not always just on the sore part!
Oh, you don't know sir, how it makes me smart!

'Oh please, sir, not on the same place again!
    Not on the same place! Oh, sir! Please, sir! pray!'
But Edgar's [tears] & [...] cries are vain.

Edgar's Flogging

You're a young poet that invokes the Muse;
    You made a song on Percy's flogging once;
Let's hear you sing it now, sir; 'tis my wish
To hear it — what! you're sulky, [...] Swish!

'Let's hear the lines on Charlie's bottom [...]
    The birch should help you to remember; [...]
I'll see if I can't make you speak, though dumb;
    What was the song of Algie's flog[ging ...]
What were the verses made on Willie's [bum]
    [...] Willie's bum was whipped to-day
With [...]
Can't you [remember ...]

The first [line] [...] was whipped to-day
    [...] you [...]
[...] Willie's bum was whipped [...]
    [...]
[...] to the birch & to the block [...]
    [...]
Of Edgar's bottom [...]
[...] than on Freddy.

But that [...]
    [...]
And now my birch is over the young poet
    I want to [hear] it from its author's [...]
Your bum was white you weren't ashamed to [...]
    I heard you say so when you stood [...]
The [fellows] bathing — but you'd ne'er have stripped
Had it been whipped as Willie's bum was whipped.

Edgar's Flogging

Still on the tenderest part the birch-twigs play
And though the sore flesh shoot [fresh …] of pain.
'It hurts you, doesn't it? don't it hurt you, eh?
It hurts you most where first the blood was drawn,
Eh, don't it, sir? did that cut sting well, Vaughan?

'Henceforward you'll not be so quick to mock
The little fellows when you see them stripped
Now you're a sheep of the same flock
And task the same twigs that their blood has tipped.
Now Edward sees you on the flogging-block;
Now Algernon & Charlie see you whipped;
When they were flogged they've often felt your chaff;
Swish, swish, swish, swish! it's their turn now to laugh.

'It's your turn now to cry, Vaughan — does it sting?
does the birch sting you? you that [came] to see
Algernon whipped, & thought it a fine thing
To brag that you had no such marks as he
On your bare bottom — you that used to sing
Songs on other boys that came to be
Flogged, & write […] on them & scoffing verses —
Your bottom is just like Algernon's or Percy's

'Ay, Vaughan, my boy, there's not a cut to choose
Between your bare backside & Algernon's:
Your naked bottom is as red as Hugh's
Now you've been whipped like any other dunce;

Edgar's Flogging

Well, now I think the little boys will sing
    Songs of your whipping, Edgar — songs of you
And how you writhed & cried like anything
    Each time the birch brushed your bare breech anew.
There — there — & there! Ay, Edgar, don't it sting?
    Ay, now your own bum knows the torture too
Ay, now you know what Regie's bottom feels
Or Algie's when [bestrewn] with bloody weals.

Rupert's Flogging

by

Etonensis

'Stand up, Rupert Wentworth, this instant! We'll square all accounts up to-day;
The arrears of a fortnight to settle — come here, Master Rupert, I say!
Now look at this list of offences — "twice late — neither lesson nor saw
Out of bounds — out of bounds" — how the birch-twigs will sting Rupert Wentworth's bare bum!
"Seven faults in his exercise" — seven! I'll correct [then] all seven in a [...]
[...] Oh! how the birch that's now soaking in brine will write out the whole list on his rump!'
Rupert Wentworth arose with a tear in his eye & a blush on his cheek:
'Tis the fourth time that Rupert has bared his posteriors for flogging this week:
His flesh is as red as an apple, but redder by far than his cheek
Are the round fleshy parts that have three times already been tickled this week.
His hair is a mass of short tangled red curls, but his eyes are dark brown —
'Go down, sir! Go down when I tell you! Go down, I say, Wentworth! Go down!'
But Wentworth stands motionless, holding his [breeches] still [up]
with both hands
He looks at the birch, & he looks at the block, & he [shrinks] where he stands.
'Come, Percy, come, Edward, & hold him — come, Charlie — come Algernon — come:
You shall all see the [battle] between a birch rod & a naughty [boy's] bum.
Here's a rod for a big fellow's bottom — nine supple tough knotty green
switches —
Breaking bounds — breaking windows — bad language — intemperance — impertinence —" "Please, Sir —"

RUPERT'S FLOGGING.

"Well, Wentworth — what is it? what have you to say in defence of your bum?"
"Oh, the window, sir, please, was an accident, please, sir — I'm sorry, sir —" "Come!
"If that's all you can say on behalf of your bottom, you'd better be dumb,
And the punch that was brewed in your bedroom ^ at midnight — an accident too?
You shall [rue] the result of that brew, sir — the draught shall be bitter for you.
I don't know your companions — I'd flog them — as you shall be flogged — if I [knew]
But at least Rupert Wentworth shall smart for it — smart for it soundly — & wish
He had rather drink rhubarb or wormwood. Come! take up his shirt for him! Swish!
Rupert Wentworth's posteriors were red from the recent birch-rod when he rose
And unbuttoned his trousers & bared his backside — but it tingles & glows
At the bitter first taste of the cutting fresh birch-twigs so smartly applied
With a blush twice as deep — & the torture convulses his burning backside.
The naked whipped bottom writhes, heaves, & contracts itself, [...] with pain,
And burning all over, & smarting [all] through, ere it tingles again!
But it [burns, it] smarts & it tingles more terribly far than before
When the second cut falls, & draws blood from the bottom [...] so sore.
It smarts & it [burns] & it tingles, it tingles, it burns, & it smarts
As the third cut is laid on the crimsoning expanse of those [...] parts.
Each cut hurts him more than the last [cut] — & still as he [writhes] from the last
He feels that the cut [...], which makes his heart flutter so fast[,]
Will hurt him still more — & he wishes that the hour of his flogging was past.
He clenches his teeth, & he clenches his hands, & he blinks off a tear
And compresses his lips till they [whiten], & he quivers with pain — not with fear.
Swish! — Swish! — Rupert winces, & draws his breath hard — & it [sounds] like a sob.
Swish! — Swish! — Rupert flinches, & draws his lips in — & the stripes burn & throb,
Swish! — Swish! — Rupert writhes, & reflects that rebellion turns out a bad job.
Swish! — Swish! — Rupert pants, catches breath, takes his underlip tight in his teeth,
Swish! — Swish! — Rupert sobs, as the birch-twigs descend on the bottom beneath.
Swish! — Swish! — Rupert stifles a cry which, if uttered, were uttered in vain,
Swish! — Swish! — Rupert drops down his forehead, & shivers all over with pain.
Swish! — Swish! — Rupert moans in his agony, smarting yet more than [before,]
Swish! — Swish! — Rupert groans as he writhes on the whipping-block, smarting still [more.]

Rupert's Flogging.

Twenty-one are the stripes that have wealed Rupert Wentworth's backside
— and he feels
The smart of each cut & the sting of each birch-twig increase as he kneels.
Each weal is a torture, and all his bare bottom is crimsoned with weals.
Weals glow to the left of his bottom, weals tingle and burn to the right of it:
And his master takes breath, looking down on his bottom, & smiles at the sight of it.
Then, casting his eye on the birch in his hand, he looks up — gives a nod —
And Reginald [Awanley] hands him a supple stout sappy new rod.
Well soaked was the birch whose good service on Wentworth's bare bottom is done.
Well soaked & well supple with brine — at each cut of the whole twenty-one
Rupert Wentworth's posteriors acknowledged how smartly the work was begun
Rupert Wentworth's posteriors, contracted & quivering with agony, showed
How keen was the smart of the stroke on the skin — & the blood as it flowed
Here & there, where the cuts had cut deepest, & hottest the [...]
Streaked all his backside with red letters that dunces might easily [read]
Which [...] that the birch was a stinger — the flogging a flogging indeed.
But the second fresh rod, with the sap in each twig & each knot & each bud on it,
Will hurt Rupert Wentworth still more that the rod thrown aside with his [...]
The twigs are as lithe & as long & as pliant, & fresh from the brine,
And stout enough not to wear [out] till the [...] full three times nine.
Such a rod is a tickler to fish with, when schoolboys' backsides are the fish.
Rupert's bottom lies quivering beneath it, and winces, and palpitates — Swish!
'[O,] please, sir!' — 'He thought it was over!' — 'O, please, sir!' — 'He thought it was done!'
Thus whisper the boys, while their schoolfellow [cries], & they grin at the fun.
Swish! Swish! The head-master could beat — with this rod — any [...] fishing.
Swish! Swish! Rupert's bottom is getting a regular jolly good swishing.
Rupert Wentworth's great brawny red bottom, with all the great bloody red weals on it
Smarts more than it smarted before from the rod whose impression it feels on it.
Swish! High on the right side a great flake of blood as birch-twigs descend
Spins out from the boy's naked bottom. When, when will his agonies end?
Swish! Low on the left side, the naked left haunch, great crimson fresh [...]
Spurts out from young Rupert's whipped bottom: the blood on both sides now streams out.
Swish! Fiercer the master's dark eyeballs grow now than the eye of a dragon is!
Each schoolboy is thrilled by the sight of his bare-bottomed schoolfellow's agonies.
Swish! Swish! Rupert's many transgression receive [...] expiation.
Swish! Swish! — as his bottom — Swish! Swish! — now glows with renewed flagellation

RUPERT'S FLOGGING

Swish! — Swish! Rupert Wentworth's backside is as red as his schoolfellows wished
For the fun's sake, to see it, when Rupert — Swish! — Swish! — was sent up to be punished.
Swish! — Swish! His superiors in standing, no less than — Swish! — Swish! — his inferiors,
Are tickled — Swish! — Swish! — at the sight and the sound of his suffering posteriors,
Swish! — Swish! Rupert roars with the pain, as he writhes like a freshly hooked fish.
Thrice nine are the cuts, when his bottom again feels the birch on it. Swish!
'Oh! Oh!' The flogging-room echoes & rings with the sufferer's cries!
But the master demands a fresh birch —yes, a third — & the light in his eyes
Grows redder with wrath & with laughter as Algernon Collingwood brings
A birch which he takes, & applies to the bottom — which feels how it stings.
Swish! 'Oh, sir — oh please, sir!' cries Rupert. Swish! Swish! 'Oh! Oh! Oh! Sir,' again
Roars Rupert. Swish! Swish! Rupert roars at each cut on his bottom — Swish! Swish! but in vain.
Swish! Swish! Rupert roars like a bull: you can tell by his cries that he's mad with the pain. (24 more
'*Sublime flagellum*!' says Percy Loraine in a whisper to Fred,
As he watches the birch in the air & the bottom beneath it, as red
As the rosiest of roses; & Frederic responds with a nod of his head.
No boy more experienced than Frederic Loraine in the *nobile bellum*
Of bottom and birch ever smarted beneath a *sublime flagellum*.
Again & again Rupert smarts, and again and again and again.
All his life he'll remember this flogging, & wince as he thinks of it, when
Old schoolfellows meet & remind him. 'By Jove, how the birch was laid into you then
How your bottom must tingle whenever you look at a birch-tree, old fellow!
How your bottom must smart when you hear the quotation — "*sublimi flagello*"!'
The red rod rises & falls: and the bottom that smarts as it sprawls
Grows redder beneath it; and writhes as the red rod rises and falls.
Rupert's throat is convulsed with the sobs that he scarce can suppress, as he turns
His face up, imploring for mercy & streaming with tears, & discerns
No sign in his master's of pity, & shrinks from the lesson he learns —
The lesson by cut after cut after cut after cut reinforced
That it's rather too late to [repent after] you find yourself publicly horsed.
Swish! — Swish! — Rupert Wentworth — Swish! — Swish! — doesn't relish the taste of the flagellation
Quaffs now — not of wine, nor of punch. If his bottom had only a rag on, he
Would — Swish! — Swish! — feel it less; but — Swish! Swish! — he is naked, and frantic with agony.
Swish! — Swish! — Rupert feels that the rage which his master in whipping him gluts
Is scarce to be satiated — Swish! — by the largest allowance of cuts.
Swish! — Swish! Rupert howls at each cut, as the pitiless rod seems to search
All the tenderest hind parts out, & leave them on fire — set on fire by the birch.
Swish! — Swish! — How it hurts him! — Swish! — Swish! — Not a boy has the heart left to mock.
Swish! — 'Now, sir, get up!' Rupert rises, all covered with blood, from the block.
He presses his shirt to his bottom — 'Come, Wentworth, it's time to be jogging!'
Rupert sobs as he buttons his breeches, and slinks from the scene of his flogging.

The Flogging-Block.

Canto XII. Rufus's Flogging

Scene — the public flogging-room. Head Master, rod in hand; boys assembled.

Dr. Birkenshaw (in a loud voice). Rufus Rodworthy Redmayne!
Arthur (aside to Bertram). By Jove, what a name it is!
Dr. B. Rufus Rodworthy —!
Rufus. Here, sir.
Frank (aside to Willie). I say, what a shame it is!
Young Redmayne gets flogged three or four times a week
Just because when he's flogged he's too plucky to squeak.
Willie. And so awfully fair, & so awfully plump,
That the rod seems to revel on Rufus's rump.
Dr. B. Rufus Redmayne, go down; for the hundredth time.
Rufus. Oh,
Let me off, then, this once sir. Oh, do, sir!
Dr. B. No, no.
There's a score for the birch & your bottom to settle,
And I've usually found you a lad of some mettle.
Now no better match can be played in the field
Where both sides are well matched & unwilling to yield
Than the match — an experience you often have had —
Between a good rod & a mettlesome lad.
The sight of a naked & smarting young dunce
Is a sight to amuse & admonish at once —
Is a sight to remember as well as enjoy:
Go down for the hundredth time, Rufus, my boy.
Rufus (muttering between his teeth). Beastly choice!
Dr. B. Beastly choice, sir! Was that what you said?
Eh?
Rufus. Yes, sir.
Dr. B. Then, Rufus, your fiery red head
Shall be presently matched by a bottom as red.
I'll make your posteriors remember me. Come,
Take your breeches down, Rufus, & shew us your bum.

To-morrow, my lad, & for many days after,
The marks on your bum shall signal for laughter —
Ay, Rufus, at least for a fortnight to come.

(Rufus unbuttons his trousers & kneels down on the flogging-block.

There are plenty already, I see, on your bum;
One, two, three — & nice fleshy red cuts — four, five, six, —
Seven, eight cuts — nine — ten — (not enough for your tricks!)
Eleven, twelve, & thirteen — & I wish
I had laid a few more on your bottom, sir! (Swish!) (Flogs Rufus

Rufus (aside). Oh, I say, — Oh, by Jove! — he'll half kill me to-day!
(Swish! Swish!) Oh, by Jove, how it hurts! — Oh, I say!
My bottom's on fire! how it burns! Oh, by God,
What an arm he has got! And, by Jove, what a rod!
(Swish! Swish!) Oh, he'll cut my poor bum to the bone!
(Swish!) Oh, how it stings! but he shan't make me groan
If (Swish!) — my God! — I can possibly help.
(Swish! Swish!) No, please God, though, it shan't make me yelp!
(Swish! Swish!) Well, if ever I felt such a rod!
Oh, by Jove! Oh, my bottom! (Swish! Swish!) Oh, my God!

(The Head Master stops to take breath, & examines the twigs of the rod in his hand.

Dr. B. Here, one of you boys, go & fetch me at once
A fresh birch, & a good one, to tickle this dunce.
Such a fine pair of swelling posteriors — a rump
So fleshy, so chubby, so brawny, so plump —
Such magnificent buttocks as Rufus is showing —
Ought always, by rights, to be tingling & glowing
To remind by their smarting the youngster who's got 'em
That the birch is too much for the biggest boy's bottom.

(Flogs Rufus.

Arthur. A'n't he catching it!

Reginald. Don't I just know how he feels!

George. There's room on that bottom for hundreds of weals;
If the buds on each twig were a dozen, each bud
Would find place for a weal — aye, a place to draw blood.
Fat, fair, & fourteen is the sufferer who smarts
For the hundredth time now in his plump hinder parts.

Rufus's Flogging 2

Dr. B. (flogging Rufus). If my arm, Master Rodworthy Redmayne, was stronger
Your flogging should be both severer & longer:
But the muscles, I think, as it is, are quite strong enough
To give you a flogging you'll smart from quite long enough.

George (aside). And he knows that he's one of the strongest men living,
And that no one could give a boy more than he's giving.
Well, hit, sir! (Seeing Rufus's bottom whipped till the blood comes.

Rufus (aside, wincing with pain). By Jove, it hurts worse than before —
The first rod hurts much, but the second hurts more;
And my bottom is all so confoundedly sore.
Oh, by Jove! — Oh, I say! was there ever a cove
So unlucky as I am! (Swish! Swish!) Oh, by Jove!

Dr. B. (smiling). Master Redmayne's posteriors, I see, are as tender
As plump — though so hardened & old an offender
Might by this time be almost expected to find
His skin, by much whipping, quite hardened behind.
But tho' all his backside is well seamed, & well scarred,
The skin is still tender, I see, & not hard.
Don't flinch, Master Rufus — don't sir! not an inch! for
If you do, sir, I'll (Swish!) give you something to flinch for —
(Flogs Rufus.

Now, Rufus, my lad, can you tell me now, come,
Was the bum made for birch, or was birch for the bum?
Was the bottom by provident nature designed
That the birch might have matter to work on behind,
Or the birch providentially made for the part
Where it constantly makes all young gentlemen smart?
Should you guess, Master Rufus, that nature or God
First moulded the bottom — then thought of the rod?
Or after the birch, with its spreading green sprays,
Lithe twigs, & tough shoots, & tough buds, met the gaze
And approval (no doubt!) of its fashioner — eh? —
Did the sight not suggest its right use — the one way
To make it of service, boy? What should you say?
Was the very first bottom — the very first boy
Ever born — made on purpose to find it employ?

Was that first born of bottoms as chubby, I wonder,
As yours is? I doubt it: conjecture might blunder.
It's well, on the whole, you're a bad boy: for were you
A good boy, it wouldn't be easy to spare you.
It wouldn't, I may say, be proper to spare
So invitingly brawny a bottom, when bare:
So temptingly chubby a bottom as yours
Provokes the infliction it braves & endures:
Such a bum seems to challenge the birch that it feels
To cover its nakedness — covered with weals.
Its natural nakedness, covered with recent
Great bloody red weals, is no longer indecent;
The sight is improving & wholesome: I wish
It may prove so to all of your schoolfellows. **Swish!**
(Flogs Rufus soundly[.]
I trust it may always impress them profoundly
To see a big boy's bottom flogged soundly.

The Flogging-Block.

www.ingramcontent.com/pod-product-compliance
Lightning Source LLC
Chambersburg PA
CBHW081232170426
43198CB00017B/2736
9780987095695